W9-CAJ-702
Homer, AK 99000-0007

Crossroads

Women Coming of Age
in Today's Uganda

Edited by Christopher Conte
Individual Contributions © The authors
2015

Individual Chapters Copyright © 2015 By Each Author
All rights reserved.

ISBN: 1507680228
ISBN 13: 9781507680223
Library of Congress Control Number: 2015901410
CreateSpace Independent Publishing Platform
North Charleston, South Carolina

Contents

Cover art: "Secret Admirer" by Ronnie Ogwang

Introduction

In 2008, not long after I began a stint as a journalist in Uganda, a Kampala-based newspaper reporter named Lydia Namubiru regaled me with stories about her life. I was spellbound. Our conversation became a running dialogue, and being journalists, we ultimately decided to collect stories like hers and publish them. Others joined the project along the way, and the result is the collection you now see before you.

Our goal was to illuminate a culture through autobiography. I had no interest in producing yet another travelogue in which an outsider would dissect Africa, and the authors wanted no part in any attempt to fit African stories to stereotypes that depict the continent as either long suffering and helpless (and hence in need of rescue) or as somehow noble and attached to nature (and hence the envy of some people in the "developed" world). Instead, we hoped that stories by "ordinary" people, told in the straight-forward manner of journalism, would offer readers more authentic glimpses into one small corner of a huge and diverse continent that is neither as pitiful nor as romantic as the stereotypes suggest.

The stories here definitely shatter stereotypes. The authors bring a fresh perspective to topics ranging from religion and politics to sports and health. They describe highly varied efforts to understand and define women's identities and changing social roles, but also examine such concerns as the rule of law, education and the pervasive influence of western culture. There is nothing abstract or theoretical about these essays, though; in profoundly personal and heart-felt ways, the authors show how these issues play out in their daily lives.

Westerners may find the stories at times surprising because they are *not* surprising; from the mother who frets about her children's schooling to the older woman who nostalgically remembers the good old days, these women seem remarkably like their sisters in America or Europe. But the differences are significant, too, and all the more enlightening because the authors describe them with critical but loving understanding. In the process, they challenge outsiders to examine their own attitudes and customs with similar objectivity.

I hope Ugandan readers also will find the essays enlightening. By shining a light on their own culture, the authors may advance the kind of conversation that any people must have about how to preserve valuable traditions – and defend them from western encroachment – while helping culture adjust to changing times.

I will be eternally grateful to the authors for the opportunity they have given me to be part of their lives. Special thanks go to Lydia Namubiru, the inspiration for the book and my guide in all things Ugandan (and many things western); to Hilda Twongyeirwe, who connected me to a world of women writers beyond the circle of journalists I knew, and who provided wise and soothing advice in times of stress; to Carol Ariba, who captured many of the book's themes with her keen eye, and who gave the book its title; to Peace Twine and others who showed the courage to discuss uncomfortable topics; and, indeed, to all the writers, who brought insight, honesty and grace to this cross-cultural collaboration.

Christopher Conte
February 2015

My Name

By Nakisanze Segawa

"My name is Nakisanze Segawa."

That has always been my response whenever I get introduced to people. With an inquisitive stare as though I have left out vital information, they ask: "Your *full* name or your other name?"

"That *is* my name," I always insist, irritated but at the same time pitying the people who ask because I already know I am not going to give them what they want: my *western* name – my religious name. But can't one be a Christian or a Muslim without borrowing a name from the western or Islamic worlds?

I remember once I was in a long queue at Rubaga Hospital, one of the two oldest hospitals in Uganda. It was started by Catholic missionaries in the early days of colonialism. I was waiting to be registered as an out-patient. When I finally reached the cashier after an hour of pushing against other patients and sharing air with a child whose heavy cough sounded like the cry of a male buffalo, the cashier refused to put my name down in the register because I did not have a religious one.

"These computers were set to start with Christian names," she said, looking at me with eyes so weary, showing every minute of her sixty-something years.

Here we go again, I thought, telling myself that I wasn't about to satisfy her. I had experienced this before in Mulago Hospital, and I wasn't going there again. "Put my name down please," I said gently, though I was aggravated. I know I should have gotten used to this situation, but I guess it's hard to get used to odd things, and besides not having a Western name, I have one male and one female name, which is odd for a girl.

"This computer will not accept these two traditional names, so tell me your other name," she demanded, frowning with a glare so piercing that for a second I thought she would slap my lips shut.

"What if I was a Muslim? Would it refuse to accept my Arabic name also?" I asked, taking in the lines on her face. She must have been born before Uganda won its independence, I thought. She probably was my grandmother's age, making her part of the generation that still thinks everything that came with the missionaries is perfect. It wouldn't surprise me to learn that she was taught by white missionaries who believed in assimilation policy: Be like a white man, have his name, speak his language, perhaps change your skin tone to match his, and of course adopt his foreign name to prove to him that you have accepted Christ.

"Don't play smart with me, young lady. If you don't have a religious name, I will not register you." She looked past my shoulders, and called out, "Next?"

"Mulindwa Muwonge," I said. Refusing to be ignored, I cited the name of the popular radio presenter to challenge her. "Does he have a foreign name? Would you refuse to register him because he doesn't have a foreign name?"

"Don't you talk to me about Mulindwa Muwonge; I know his family well. He was born a Muslim. Next?"

"I am not moving until I get registered," I asserted, my voice pitched high.

"Why don't you just tell her your muzungu name?" Asked a woman behind me, I turned and looked at her. She was the one who had come with the coughing child. She appeared to be younger than I, probably 19 or 20 years.

"I have already told her my name. Do I have to pull out my voting card for her eyes?"

"Do you practice witchcraft?"

"She must. It's the only explanation," said the cashier, joining in the insult.

I looked back at the cashier, and waited for her to make up her mind.

"Why can't you just register her?" asked a man who was behind the woman with the coughing child. "Where was it written in the Bible or the Quran that one should have a muzungu or Arab name? Or, rather, is it written anywhere in the constitution of the country? The young lady has come here to be treated, not to get interrogated. And you, the cashier, should focus on doing what brings food to your grandchildren's table."

The cashier finally relented. "What is your name?" she sighed.

I smiled when she handled me the payment receipt with my full name on it: Nakisanze Segawa.

I was raised Nakisanze Joyce and kept those names until I was introduced to literature – specifically, to African literature. If it were not for books, I wouldn't have dropped my western name and had these unusual conflicts. The first book I read was *Ebyedda Bissasika*, Chinua Achebe's classic *Things Fall Apart*, translated into my native language, Luganda. I was thrilled by the major character, Obi, but even more by the writer, who is Nigerian. How could a person put words together in such a thrilling way, forming beautiful, long roads on white paper? I wanted to be like that person. So I looked for ways to be like him, for something that I could have in common with him. That is when I decided to drop the name Joyce. I never liked it anyway because almost all the women who sold locally-made alcohol in my community happened to be named Joyce. So I replaced it with my father's name, Segawa.

A year later, I read *The River Between,* a classic by the Kenyan author Ngugi wa Thiong'o, who was baptized James Ngugi, but later dropped his Christian name. I fell in love. It was the first literary African romance that I had come across. So now, I had two favorite writers, and neither had a western name. I was going to share their passion. Someday I was going to write, and the name on my stories, as well as on my education and legal documents, would be Nakisanze Segawa.

In Uganda, people assume everyone with a Christian name to be a Christian. Now that I no longer have a Christian name, people have to ask my religion. My answer is and has always been that I am a Christian.

"But you don't have a Christian name." they say.

"If Jesus' other name wasn't Christ, would it have made a difference?"

"What are you trying to say?"

"What is in a name?"

"It denotes recognition and one's identity without requiring any further question."

"But it also triggers divisions, prejudice and discrimination amongst human kind, especially in people of the same race or nationality. For instance, we may both be of the same ethnicity, but you might have a problem relating to me because my name is Rita and yours is Muhammad."

At the age of five, I was introduced to the woman who was to raise me as her own child for the next nine years. In my first years under her guidance, she took us children with her to the Adventist church. I later learned that she was born to Muslim parents. That automatically made her a Mohammedan at birth. But she stopped going to the mosque, and converted to Christianity. Later, she stopped going to church too, and became more involved in running her own business, which she opened every day of the week.

My stepmother had a fever for money, and wanted passionately to succeed in life on her own. This eventually led her to the path of the traditional gods. She started smoking *emindi*, the traditional smoking pipe, an act commonly seen as a way to seek guidance and fulfillment of worldly desires from the ancestral gods. I remember watching her puff at the *emindi*, and exhale the smoke through her nose and slightly parted lips. The smoke rose up into the dark space. I imagined it was wandering in the air until it reached the gods. I remember wondering why she was doing this evil act. Anything that involves consulting the ancestral gods is perceived by most Ugandans as satanic. This attitude was planted by missionaries; in most cases, traditional culture and Christianity or Islam do not mix.

Eventually, her finances got better. She bought her own land, built her own house and managed to keep in school the four children she had before she married my *taata* (father). She liked to tell stories of witchcraft and of how one of her brothers occasionally ran mad because he had refused to serve the gods. It was then that I started believing that the gods were present and powerful in people's lives. I remember being fascinated by her stories. Perhaps it's then that I started questioning Christianity.

I never saw my biological mother go to church; I guess she wasn't accustomed to the ritual when still young. In fact, I neither heard her talk about traditional religion with disapproval nor praise Christianity, though she took her brother's children to church for Holy Communion. However, she often was glued to a certain radio show – I don't remember its name – that was mainly about religious differences between Muslims, Pentecostals and traditionalists. Each group claimed to be the true religion. My mother loved the traditionalist on the panel, who kept saying that the gods we please will choose us to go to heaven. But she also loved to put God in her words. She was a sickly woman who seldom left her room by the time I went back to live with her in 2002, at sixteen. My stepmother had long left *Taata*, and he had become a depressed, angry and sickly man. I could no longer live with him. I think I gave my mother the worst but also the happiest days of her life. She was happy to live with me once again, even though I had come to her with all the baggage that comes with being a teenager. I made her cry many times about many things, but she always forgave me.

I tell my friends that I am a Christian but with little faith in the Lord Jesus. He doesn't speak to me as strongly as the mountains, the rivers, the lakes, the valleys, the forests and the gentle and wild beasts of the earth. When I look at these natural beauties and think of the invisible force behind their creation (just as my ancestors who believed in the Supreme Being, the creator of everything on earth, did), I say amen to God. I might sound confused, but I am sure I am not because I know that all religions, whatever their legends, acknowledge the existence of an omnipotent force far stronger than the gods and fellow humans who once lived among us as Jesus did. When I think of the creator of heaven and earth, the theory of trinity loses its meaning, for there is no way the most Supreme Being would wish to be equated to his son or another of his creations.

My friends believe I am crazy, that I think too much, that faith is supposed to be blind. But how am I supposed to be blind when the creator of everything wonderful gave me the eyes to see and the brain to analyze and question? I have respect for all religions on earth, as long as they respect the laws of the biblical Ten Commandments, which are alive in my understanding of order. So long as we believe in humanity and treat each other with fairness and equality, things like names, religion, gender, age, race and ethnicity have little meaning. As I grow older, I question my Christianity and slowly understand and value traditional beliefs. Perhaps my friends are right. If I don't believe that much in Christ as I should but instead embrace the Old Testament more, then I am not a Christian. Yet I do believe in the Bible, and refer to it more and more each day. At the same time, just as my two mothers, I keep telling myself that perhaps one day, I too will visit the shrine and consult the gods.

So here I am. In Uganda, it's assumed that everyone with a western name is a Christian, everyone with an Arabic name is a Muslim, and everyone with only traditional names is linked to traditionalism – and, hence, is backward and evil. But I do not like people to make such assumptions about me. The two women who raised me never read books and had little education – I don't think either got past primary four – but each told me in these exact words: "Be whatever you want to be. Go wherever your fantasies take you, as long as that place exists."

For me, that place is in the literary world, where my name won't trigger any evil suspicions, and I will be accepted for what I am, just like Chinua and Ngugi.

My name is Nakisanze Segawa.

Crossroads

By Caroline Ariba

I am a Ugandan woman, and proud to be one. I went to school and earned a college degree. I can speak and write in the white man's language – more fluently, in fact, than I can speak in my own language. No one can take that from me. In Uganda, having an education like mine means you are modern, strong and reborn. Women who never had the chance to be educated view you as a dream from which they would never want to wake. But time and again, I find myself wondering: Am I any different from less fortunate Ugandan women?

For a long time, I thought there is no way we could ever be similar. I rarely break a sweat, frequently sleep in, and earn my bread by typing words on a computer. My poorer counterparts wake up in the wee hours, run to the garden, rush back home to prepare breakfast, run back to the garden, return to prepare lunch, and in the evening after a harsh day of toil, the only thanks they might get is a beating from their husbands. That just can't be me, no way. Or at least that's what I have told myself.

The rural Ugandan woman goes through life by one rule: culture. She is born into a series of laws made by our forefathers on how girls should behave. I have often told myself that I dodged the bullet. But did I? Once, when I was in a small health center called Wera in the eastern district of Amuria, I met Acom, a woman who had just had a baby. It was her fifth child in six years, but she wasn't finished yet. All of her babies, including this new one, were girls, and she desperately needed a baby boy. Otherwise, she and her children would inherit nothing. Only a baby boy would save the day. That's what my culture says.

There she sat – all worn out and sore, newborn baby girl in her arms. Instead of wearing a smile, she was sad. When she left the hospital, she would have to brave the long walk home. If her baby had been a boy, her husband would have picked her up. He already had married another woman who bore him sons. If he were to die, Acom would be left with nothing except maybe a little space for her tiny hut. She had nowhere to go. Marriage is all she knew, and her girls were born into a home where everyone wished they were something different. She knew she had to keep trying to produce a male heir – or die trying.

This lady is nowhere near my league, I thought. But in reality, we are one. The only way I can ever own my father's property is if my brothers let me, since they own all the land that previously was passed on to my father by his father. Never mind that women take care of the land and do all the donkey work. The silent yet deep law of tradition requires that girls get only what boys toss their way. There are some exceptions, of course, but even the women who inherit property must endure resistance from their uncles.

As I pitied this woman lying so forlorn in the hospital, I wondered: Are the men I date different from her traditional husband? Once, a guy told me he wanted to have more boys than girls. If he struggles to build his empire, he explained, it only makes sense to pass it on to his son because girls get married and forget their families. The modern woman in me fled for the hills, but a tiny bit of me thought I surely wouldn't fail to get this guy a son if we got married. Otherwise, he might try for a son outside of marriage.

I don't really blame him. Culture guides us all. Whether we like it or not, many of us celebrate the birth of a girl only if a boy already has arrived. Sometimes, you find children whom whole neighborhoods call "Boy." Most of the times, when you look at these toddlers' families, you find that the boy was born after many girls, and his birth so overjoyed everyone they gave him the simple nickname, "Boy."

Culture has its claws deep into us from the time we are born. It teaches us that fear often is interpreted as respect. Lately, the media have been awash with stories about a ban on corporal punishment in schools and homes. While talk about alternative forms of punishment is long overdue, I wonder if anything will change. In rural areas, there are women who think that a beating from their husbands is a sign of love. Imagine what such women do with their children. Often, they show their children affection only for the first few months of life. After that, tough love begins.

I was raised by a very strong woman, but she was overwhelmed by her many children. We called her all sorts of names like "the lioness." We feared her. No one wanted to be on her wrong side lest she would unleash the "rod of correction" on us. That's what the Bible calls a few strokes of the cane. Personally, I got the cane mostly from people who took care of us, not my mum. But the relationship between my brothers and her was often war.

Once, they went swimming in a local river that was notorious for drowning. When she found out, she threw some lashes of the cane their way. But they were defiant. After their punishment, they walked out of the room laughing, and the rest of us gathered around to see the marks, or "accessories," that the beatings left on their bodies. One pointed to a welt on his wrist and said his "accessory" was "a watch." Another boasted that he had a new "belt."

In retrospect, Mum's beatings may have served mainly to teach my brothers how to block pain. That ability came in handy at school, where we were beaten for the tiniest of reasons. Sometimes, we didn't even know why we were beaten. There was no guessing when the cane would come; we were beaten in school nearly every day.

In this cruel world, my elder brother emerged a hero. No beating moved him. He never cried, never even flinched. One time, an English teacher decided to beat the whole class for making noise, starting with my brother. After three strokes of the cane, the boy just lay there smiling. Harder and harder the teacher beat, but to no end. Frustrated, the teacher threw the cane down and walked away. My brother had won. After that, the class always begged my brother to go first when there was a punishment.

I, on the other hand, was a big coward until I improvised a means to reduce the pain. I would pack an exercise book in my panties, or put on extra clothes to protect myself as best I could. Others pursued the same strategy. In fact, skinny children seemed to put on weight once a new school term began because they were stuffed with exercise books and extra clothes.

We adapted in other ways too. At one point, the children in school gave their canings medicinal names. If you got three strokes of the cane, the first would be paracetamol, the second aspirin, and the third chloroquine. It became a joke. Some of us even preferred beatings to alternative punishments, like frog jumping, in which miscreants were required to hop across the school yard like frogs. That could be exhausting. Teachers and parents seemed to prefer beating too; they found it quick and easy.

But the beatings led us astray. We were not learning. We feared speaking up. When I joined high school, the canes at home stopped, but the ones in school intensified. I mastered survival by holding in my feelings. I learned to speak only when I had to, and to fake happiness. When I was angry, I cried in the dark, and spoke only when I was choking with emotion. Later, when the canes stopped, I finally learned to voice my thoughts. But it was difficult at first; the first time, I could only do so through a letter.

I don't know about the long-term effect beating had on my brothers. I would like to believe they just don't care. In this part of the world, only two things break men: women and money.

Would I beat my children or tolerate a school that did? Hell no! At least, that's what I tell myself. Most of today's parents know the importance of taking time to talk to their children. Our parents didn't know that, no one taught them in any way other than with "tough love." But my generation doesn't have all the answers. It takes imagination and experience. Sometimes I think the way to discipline boys is to deny them food. Caning never worked with my brothers; I don't remember seeing any of them shed tears when they were beaten. But when someone tampered with their favorite meal, they cried like babies.

In the western world, some parents "ground" misbehaving children. But in my part of the world, if Mum had told me I was grounded, I would have been in heaven. Especially in rural areas, where there is no TV, no video games, nothing, what privileges can a parent revoke?

So I wonder. Would I defy tradition, or would I follow it? One part of me says, "Woman, you are above this," but the other wonders, "Really?" I am a stable person, but am I that way because I was beaten or in spite of it? I am supposed to be the strong, literate and self-assured African woman, but I can't quite resolve the debate in my mind.

Uganda is a multi-cultural country, but most of our traditions have at least one thing in common: They all hold that women should be submissive. Girls are supposed to kneel before their elders, and wives are supposed to kneel before their husbands. I am above that . . . at least I should be above that. But am I? My knees are dark from all the kneeling I have done – to take men water for washing hands, to greet them, to show them respect. While I was growing up, even my mum refused to kneel because she thought it was belittling. But I have failed to find the strength to defy tradition. So I argue with myself. Often, I end up with a compromise – an awkward curtsy, somewhere between standing and kneeling. "Just as long as my knees don't touch the ground," I tell myself.

Kneeling is the tiniest of my conflicts. Recently, my sister got married. We come from a culture that believes the groom's family should pay the bride's family for her. No matter how modern the family, the love your husband has for you is measured by the number of cows he brings as bride price. So there on my sister's wedding day were my uncles and the in-laws arguing over the worth of this beautiful and intelligent woman. I thought to myself, "My sister is priceless. Where would I start if I had to say how many cows she was worth? And how many cows would be a fitting price for me?"

Haggling over bride price reaches a peak during the marriage ceremony. After the food has been served, the in-laws and bride's family meet. That is when you hear the banging of tables and bitter exchanges of words. When everyone eventually emerges, no one has a happy face.

As bad as I feel for the bride being valued in terms of cattle, I pity the groom and his family too. Prior to the traditional marriage, they meet with the bride's family to learn its demands. In many cases, the grooms vanish in thin air when the demands are too much. At the wedding, the groom is expected to bring not only the dowry but gifts for the bride's family, including fancy traditional wear for her parents, aunties, uncles and brothers. He also must carry some food for the girl's parents as a way of saying thank you for raising his wife to be. My grandfather had 13 wives and more than 50 children. My sister chose a few aunties and uncles to receive gifts, but many others thought they deserved largesse too.

The groom also has to buy his bride a suitcase full of accessories and clothes that he hands over at the wedding. And during the course of the event, the bride's clan shows off their other girls to potential in-laws; as they leave, the groom is expected to give each an envelope filled with money. It is understandable if the groom can't meet everybody's expectations, but many will think he loves his bride less if he doesn't.

Why should culture cost that much? Why should love be measured by such standards? Are we that petty? If I love someone, how could I put him and his family through that kind of stress and embarrassment?

I thought my assertive sister, who doesn't let people take her for granted, would not let people treat her like an inanimate art piece or tear her man down with demands. But society doesn't view a woman as fully married unless she honors these customs. My sister bowed to custom, and today she is happy.

My other sister is happy too, though. She opted to ignore the demands of culture. She simply went to court in a hush-hush ceremony, and married the father of her kids. Do I think she was brave? Of course, I do. Do I think she wishes it were different? I can't tell. Her lovely and healthy babies, who run around with big smiles, erase many doubts. But the elders believe she isn't married. Other village folk consider her relationship loveless. And if her husband ever decides to marry her in the traditional way, he will have to pay an extra cow or more for each of his own children since they are considered to belong to the woman's clan until a man pays dowry bride price for their mother.

Whenever I visit my sisters, I am at peace with myself, satisfied with whatever course I may choose or hopeful that somehow I will find a middle way. But when I am alone with my thoughts, I wonder: What I should do?

Sometimes I think I could leave Uganda in a heartbeat and never look back. It can seem so God-forsaken. Besides cultural beliefs and traditions that sadden me, I am heartsick at its poverty and the hard lives so many of my countrymen live. But some things will always draw me back. Its dance. Its songs. Its wonderful instruments. The way the drums summon all and sundry, and how the dancing women tease the men, and the men act all macho in return. The women are in control, and the men dance to their every tune while keeping their manliness intact.

When the party is done, we have wondrous funerals. I don't understand the way the white man mourns. I just don't. All in black, big hats on their heads, hands neatly tucked, tears quickly brushed away. That is just sad! When we lose a person, we mourn hard until we have no tears left. Forget the part where we try to be modern, wear black outfits and mourn quietly. We bury our dead in the soil of their families' ancestral land. People gather from far and wide. Culture requires togetherness in times like this, and mourners often stay for a week or more. At night, there are not enough beds, so people sleep everywhere and anywhere. Sitting rooms are a pile of people, feet and faces easily blending. No one really cares. Outside, on the ground, under the trees, everywhere – people sit, sleep, lie and sing, just being there for each other. When a woman arrives, she announces herself with a long, loud wail about how the person's death has left her empty. Others may join her wailing with abandon.

And the songs! Every tribe in Uganda has a mourning tune, usually written by village women. They voice words of praise to the dead. Even when the tears are not flowing, we eloquently express our sorrow with song.

We mourn until we can laugh. Once at a particularly painful funeral for an uncle of mine, mourners were asked to drop their offerings in a basket placed next to the coffin when they came for the last viewing. A mentally unstable woman appeared, obviously saddened by my uncle's death. As she approached the body for her last viewing, she became animated, singing all kinds of praise for the deceased. She picked a coin from her pocket, but instead of putting it in the basket, she put it on the coffin.

As she walked away, she suddenly stopped, and then started howling insults at the dead man. She ran back and grabbed her coin, saying that, after all, he was dead, and she needed it more. She was back to her crazy self, and she was on fire. She sat next to a couple of old women who were wailing. Looking quizzically at them, she asked loudly, "Why are you crying? I hear the food is even not enough. Why waste your energy?" Suddenly, the crowd's wailing turned into laughter. In fact, we laughed our tears dry. Later that night, we sat around the fire telling stories, bathing in warmth and togetherness.

This mentally unstable woman captured an inescapable truth about burials: Many people attend in anticipation of a good meal. Burial is food time. Once, after we buried a nephew of mine, I was sitting with family and friends when a little girl walked up to her mother. Her belly, shiny and marked where soup had run across it, was so full she could barely walk. "Mummy, I have eaten a lot of rice," she boasted, unconsciously mirroring the similarly-sated adults nearby. We burst out laughing, and for a while, the pain was gone. Even as we painfully lay our loved ones to rest, we spare a moment to laugh the pain away.

I am a university graduate. I should be able to say no to my culture, to be free to do as I please. But no, not everything I do is of my volition. Sometimes I can't fathom the decisions I make. I keep thinking I am different from traditional Ugandan women. My English may be well beyond the "yes" and "no" that is all some rural women can say. But on another, perhaps more important level, I speak the same language as the women who can barely read and write. Is that freedom? I don't know. What I know is that I can never raise my voice and declare that I am a modern woman with no trace of tradition. Every day is a battle that I may never resolve. I will always be a Ugandan.

God's Mistake or Mine?

By Rosey Sembatya

When I turned 10 I wanted to be a boy. It had nothing to do with wanting to inherit my father's property. Rather, I wanted the liberties that came with boys' clothing. Shorts especially had an allure. When I saw boys my age squat with their knees touching their chins without anyone scolding them or telling them to sit "properly," I felt envy. I was convinced I was missing all the fun.

I was raised hearing that "A girl is supposed to be tender," as my mother would say. "Some games are so male that they would rob a girl of her worth," the mantra continued. But fun for me was in play and laughter, not skirts and dresses that seemed to be designed to nip the fun. With fury starting to boil, I learned in Sunday school that God is the Ultimate – nothing is beyond His power. But I also learned that God can make mistakes, and in His power can unmake them too. No amount of telling would convince me that I was meant to be a girl – tender, lovely, meek, my father's jewel. While my arms would bruise when pressed hard and my play toys were dolls – plastic Barbies whose eyes would dance in their sockets and ones made of banana fiber with frail arms and neither eyes nor hair – nothing could deter me from praying to God to change me to a boy.

Houses in our neighborhood were built close to each other, and there were many children, so play was always exciting. Different homes were our play arenas. Nancy's home had a lot of *passplum* – grass that adults nurtured like babies. This is where we would play dodge ball, thereafter watering the trampled grass so that it would miraculously grow back before Nancy's parents got home. When we weren't playing dodge ball, there is a good chance we would be found climbing trees in the neighborhood, although this, too, was considered wrong for a dress-wearing girl.

My family's compound had one significant play place, an anthill. We could climb to the top and see Lake Victoria. But what most interested us was the descent. Nancy, my sisters and I would take turns sitting in a half jerry can and riding down. This was very difficult to do in the dresses and skirts that we had to wear. We had to fold them carefully so that we could sit in a "proper" position. Repeated trips down the anthill would wear holes in our clothes, making it difficult to hide our passion for this most exciting game. Our parents hated it, though. I was to learn later they were concerned about protecting our tenderness, and thus preparing us to be submissive and worthy of protection by men.

As the years rolled, my friends and I talked about God. Our juvenile conversations often focused on His mistakes. For instance, we attributed big noses to periodic surpluses of clay; God had no choice but to "waste" the excess by giving an occasional person a big nose. Smaller noses, on the other hand, resulted when God was in a hurry to embark on a journey. We would discuss where God would travel, mentioning places our teacher had discussed in social studies lessons – Hong Kong, America, Seychelles or Robben Island. Other times, we figured God went to Zanzibar for cowrie shells or to Egypt for the pyramids.

From such speculation, we would move on to trying to decipher God's character. We would ask what He would do if we forgot to pray before we ate or if one of us pinched another in the dark. These conversations would progress to Hulk Hogan, the Undertaker in television's *Wrestle Mania* and our favorite movie, *Deadly Prey*. We would re-enact the films, taking turns playing different roles, deciding who would be the enemy, who would die and who would be the indomitable star.

But amidst all the fun lay a serious concern. I resolved to get to the bottom of God's mistake in making me a girl. I was born after a long drought of girl children in my family. My father had been anxious for girls, and when my older sister came before I did, he wanted even more girls. I appeared, answering his prayers.

I was 10 when I started trying not to be a girl. This stage of my life started with the realization that I could not squat as I pleased because it was a taboo for a girl to allow her knees to touch her chin. To me, squatting was almost a hobby, a stance so natural it was like a reflex. But reprimands from elders kept pushing me to distrust this reflex.

I also developed a strong dislike for skirts. They limited my freedom at play. During our play movies, it was difficult to die in a skirt or dress; people in their death throes are not supposed to have girlish manners but to perish as dramatically as possible, thrown against a wall or with legs splayed in a decidedly unfeminine way. How I hated the dress I had to wear to school – a blue, checked costume that stopped at the shin, coupled with grey stockings that were to be worn in their full glory almost all the way up to the knees. This garb made squatting difficult, to say the least.

When I was growing up, I also noticed that some colors were gender-specific. White was the epitome of cleanliness, and therefore was assigned to the "F" sex. Colors like brown, black and grey were considered male. These dull colors had decided practical advantages. My pink, light blue or white knickers were invariably more difficult to keep clean. Dresses and skirts would be long and such a burden that had they been words, they would have been called a mouthful. Washing them became a nightmare that kept me busy long after my brothers were done with their own cleaning. That irked me, and strengthened my resolve to become a boy.

What sparked this desire cannot be pinned to a particular incident, but it eventually found focus in my love for shorts. My mother was reluctant to buy me shorts because they tempt one to stretch one's legs. In shorts, one can be confident that even while dying dramatically in a movie everything that should be kept under wraps won't see the light of day.

And so, the early years of my second decade began and ended with fervent checks every night and morning for an answer to my prayers for an outer growth, an inkling of a forming organ, a new year's present from God. I believed Him capable of such surprises and more. Each year ended with hope and a resolve to make my prayers more consistent, to become more kind to others and to attend church every Sunday, if only to show God that this was serious and needed His immediate attention.

But God took his time, and slowly led me to a change of heart. First, he delayed my menses. While other girls in my class whispered that they had "seen the moon," and had notes to compare, mine didn't show up for another two years. Ashamed to be falling behind my peers, I had to invent stories, feign cramps, carry Panadols to flaunt and even fake tantrums for good measure. It paid off because I remember several whispers intimating that "it is that time of the month" to explain my moody behavior.

Such moments remind me of the senior lady at school, the one who carried a whip and could smell a pregnancy from afar simply by staring intently into a girl's eyes. She was the face of terror, known only by her title. Somehow she knew I had neither experienced the intricacies of being a female nor celebrated it. I would wonder how she had known that my menses had taken a detour. She would smile every time I was in the inspection line. This line was like a walk of shame, for it was here that we would learn who had started showing "bad manners," a euphemism for having sexual relationships with boys. Every girl had to be on this line. But the Senior Lady would always say that I grinned "with playfulness that only lack of experience could arouse." So I could pass without question, while the rest of my ilk would be met with stern looks and a feel of their bellies and breasts followed by a feel of their pulses.

Something happens to a girl when all her classmates have had their menses except her. Something hollow that makes one feel less of a girl, agitated and apprehensive. I began fearing that God actually had answered my immature prayers. Now I didn't want Him to fulfill my earlier wishes. My prayers had changed course, and I begged God to let the menses come. And breasts too, no matter how small.

In all this fuss, people started noticing that I had a chest so flat nothing could ever grow on it. Indeed, I could wear a shirt and pass for a boy, with inch-long hair that was a prerequisite for being in school. Just like the menses, breasts had heeded my earlier, fervent prayers and remained hidden. Nor could I catch a whiff of the body changes that swell the hips or make hearts skip among the opposite sex. So love eluded me, and I slipped into desperation akin to drowning. Talk was rife of how certain insects could awaken a dead chest. I sought these out. They were rare because they chose to hide in the soil and seemed to appear on whims – sometimes after a rain, other times in the scorching sun. These little black insects had a way of stimulating the chaste nipple with a bite that felt like an oxymoron: it stung, and it was delicious.

I don't know how, but the breasts finally came, and with them the interest of the opposite sex. My transformation had finally arrived.

Now I think about why I wear skirts and dresses more than I do trousers and why I love being a woman. I think it is that women have so much power. We have power that can only compare to a tongue. I came to this realization in the most selfish of actions. I saw a collection of stories entitled *Wicked Women of the 19th Century*. That era appealed to me, and the word "wicked" had a special allure, drawing me to a roadside stall that had various collections of old newspapers, books and magazines – *Hello, Cosmopolitan, True love, Beautiful Living,* and classics like *The Tempest* and *Jane Eyre.* Such stories regaled me with how women had brought down empires and made men's hearts burn. I read stories of how some car brands celebrate women, how Margaret Thatcher calmed Gorbachev's heart, and of how the magnificent Taj Mahal was a token of a man's undying love for a woman. Later, I read Maya Angelou's *Phenomenal Woman.* My transformation was complete. I was glad I had stopped my childhood prayers.

Ssengas and the Single Woman

By Shifa Mwesigye

I had grown tired standing under the sweltering sun waiting for a woman I had only met over the phone. For a moment, my spirits lifted when a taxi appeared in the distance, but they quickly sank as it sped past, covering me in its trail of dust. I'd had enough. I had worked hard to organize my friend's bridal shower, but the ssenga I was waiting to bring to the event was nowhere to be seen.

As I turned to walk away, a woman dressed in a *gomesi*, the traditional dress of Ugandan women, drove up, and asked for directions. To my relief, she introduced herself as Ssenga Hamidah, the woman I had hired to come to the shower. My plans were not ruined after all. In fact, under the ssenga's guidance, the afternoon would turn out to be quite memorable, though not in ways I had expected. It was full of laughter, embarrassment, indignation, and, for me at least, many questions about what it means to be a woman in Uganda today.

Ssenga Hamidah represents an attempt to keep alive an ancient Ugandan tradition. By custom, ssengas are paternal aunts who assume special responsibilities much like those of godparents. But instead of being responsible for children's religious instruction, they guide their nieces in the ways of society. Ssengas teach young girls how to behave, show respect and deference to others, and always display quiet grace. On school holidays, girls usually are sent off to their families' villages or to ssengas, who monitor their manners and ways around the house – including how well they can cook traditional meals, wash, and even make beds. Eventually, ssengas prepare girls for the most important role they will play in life – to be good wives.

Ssengas also teach young virgin girls about their bodies. Occasionally a ssenga will inspect girls' knickers and beds to see how well they keep them clean. She will teach about shaving and how girls should wash their lady parts (advising, them, for instance, to use one or two fingers to clean the inside). Ssengas also teach girls about sex – most importantly stressing that they must not engage in unmarried sex with boys. When a girl falls pregnant, it concerns not only her mother, but her ssenga, who was supposed to teach her better.

Girls take their ssengas' sex education to be gospel truth because after all, what does a young girl know? Back in the day, every girl was required to remain a virgin until she married, and the only lessons she received came from her ssenga. On the day of a young bride's formal "introduction" to her husband-to-be – the ceremony when the bride's family and the groom's family meet to consecrate the union – it was the ssenga who ritualistically walked among the groom's large family and "picked" from among them the man who would be the husband. After the marriage, it was the ssenga's concern if a new wife took too long to bear children. And when the girl finally became pregnant, it was the ssenga's role to coach her through the pregnancy and after delivery.

Finally, ssengas helped make sure a girl's marriage worked. They made regular courtesy calls to the couple to make sure their charges were treating their husbands well, and if a husband was unhappy with his wife, he reported her to the ssenga. In most cases, the ssenga tried to fix the problem by sitting the wayward wife down and advising her how to treat her husband. A ssenga generally didn't even consider whether a wife had concerns about the marriage. To her, the only issue was preserving the marriage, and for that, responsibility rested almost entirely with the wife.

Because of ssengas' seniority and authority, girls generally respected their every word. At least that was the tradition. But tradition no longer has the same sway. Today, many girls grow up in broken or fatherless families, and many others have families who do not feel bound by the ways of the past. As a result, fewer and fewer girls have ssengas. Girls find role models and learn about sex on TV, and feel they have less need for ssengas.

Still, culture dies hard, and society has developed a "modern" way to keep the old ways going: We now have professional ssengas. Ssenga Hamidah was one such commercial ssenga, and her job at my friend's shower was to deliver a lesson in Ugandan culture – specifically, in how to be a wife – in two hours (if we went even an extra minute over the limit, we would have to pay for another full hour).

Ssenga Hamidah began her work quietly. When she entered the house, she sat in a corner and watched as the girls came for the event. Her observations lay the groundwork for her first lesson. The issue was manners. The ssenga noted which girls had greeted her, which ones showed enough respect to kneel as tradition dictates, and which ones had ignored her. She also pointed out which of us had nonchalantly strolled into the bride's bedroom, noting that a woman, once she is married, should not let people walk casually into her room.

All this made us a little nervous, perhaps because we recognized the truth in what she said. We had violated traditional norms.

Next, the ssenga lectured the bride-to-be on how to treat her husband. "You must kneel for him when greeting him every morning, when he returns from work and when serving him," she said. "You must be on your knees when talking to him." We had heard this before, of course. Many of our mothers knelt for men. We even had seen older women kneel for their young sons-in-law.

The ssenga went on to lecture the bride-to-be to rise each morning by 5 am to make her husband's breakfast. If he wants eggs, she should prepare every kind of egg – fried, boiled and scrambled – so that he can choose which type he wants; the rest of the family can eat what he leaves behind.

You could feel a stir in the room, and some of the young women started snickering. But the ssenga was undaunted. If you came into the marriage with a car, you should let him drive it while you make your way in taxis, even if they are hot and crowded. You must keep his clothes, shoes, socks and hankies clean and pressed. When he returns home, you must welcome him at the door, take whatever he is carrying, kneel down and thank him for all he does. When he slumps into the chair or on the bed, you must take off his shoes and socks before you dash to the kitchen to get him a glass of freshly-made juice. And he always should eat first, even before the children, because, after all, he buys the family's food.

At this, our cynicism turned to indignation. Don't we work too, get tired just as he does, and come home just as much in need of rest? Don't we have children who need our attention too? And why should we do all the household chores? What is he marrying – a maid?

Despite our hostility, the ssenga went on. In fact, the best was yet to come: Sex.

A woman should always be prepared and ready to receive her husband, the ssenga said. A husband is entitled to sex anytime he feels like it. To entice and please her man, a woman should wear beads around her waist.

As she talked, the ssenga dropped to the floor. Lying on her back, she demonstrated to us how we should act in bed. She took us through the different styles of sex, the movements that we must do. Twisting the waist, it seems, is a very important part of the game. She taught us the art of moaning in bed – evidently another core part of the act.

Our anger turned to laughter. Still the ssenga went on. After sex, she said, a wife must clean her husband. She took out four pieces of cloth to demonstrate. We were told to lay the biggest one on the bed before sex. The other three are for cleaning the man after sex. Once the man is done, the woman must get a bucket of warm water, dip in a cloth, and wipe him clean from head to toe. When he is clean and resting, she then must take a shower and clean herself in case he wants more sex sometime later in the night.

Our laughter became laced with scorn. Why doesn't *he* wash *us* or take a shower? And what if we are tired?

Her response was unsatisfying – but also unsettling: "If you don't do it, another woman will do it." In the ssenga's view, society looks at women who do not kneel as stubborn. Any woman submissive enough to kneel will probably keep peace in the home, and her husband will reward her by providing for her needs.

Abhorrent as the idea seems, kneeling does work. I have read countless articles written by Kenyan men suggesting that Ugandan women, unlike their Kenyan counterparts, get what they want from their husbands – usually without even asking. That's because Ugandans know how to manipulate their husbands into giving. Kneeling really does assuage a husband's temper; it shows that his wife is calm and respectful, and won't raise her voice against him.

The ssenga's comments may have seemed like a joke to us Kampala women, but they are – or at least have been traditionally – a serious matter. In fact, girls start preparing to please men at a tender age before they hit puberty, before starting their first menstrual period – even before they stop humming or singing "Baa-baa Black Sheep."

I was born in the Ankole tribe from western Uganda, but I was brought up in the Buganda culture of central Uganda, and was taught its values and beliefs. My father was absent, so I never had a ssenga. But I learned in school what girls with ssengas already had learned at home. One of my first lessons in womanhood involved the practice called "pulling," which has spread from the Baganda to other tribes as well.

My first teachers were other girls. One night after crawling into bed at my boarding school, I heard a group of older girls quietly talking about how their ssengas had taught them to "visit the bush" and "pull." I did not understand, but I listened intently while pretending to be asleep under my covers. It turned out one of the older girls also did not know what pulling was. So they called a younger girl forward and told her to undress and lie down with her legs apart. Then, an older girl pointed out the *labia minora*. Every day, she said, a girl had to tug these two flaps of skin, which are found on either side of the opening of the vagina, until they were stretched to the equivalent of the length of the middle finger. So this, I thought as I hid under the covers, was "pulling."

On another night I got to witness the practice. It was way past lights-out time. The older girls again came into their corner, this time carrying herbs, which they crushed with their palms. Then they undressed, sat down with candles between their legs, applied the herbs to their private parts and started pulling. Some were helping each other. They looked as if they were milking cows. Those who were a bit shy stayed in bed and performed the act under the covers.

Soon I, too, was told to start visiting the bush. Just as society invented commercial ssengas to fill in where actual ones were unavailable, it seems schools filled the breach for girls who had no ssengas to initiate them in the art of pulling. This became clear when the school's headmistress took the younger girls aside, and gave us a lecture. She said all our mothers, grandmothers, sisters and neighbors had pulled, and it was our duty to do the same. Then she took us to a small garden of herbs, showed us which herbs to pick, how to grind them until they became moist and soft, and how to hold them against the labia and pull.

I resolved never to take part in this repulsive act. When I looked down at myself, there was barely anything to hold and pull. It would be painful and unbearable, like trying to grab the tight skin at the corner of your mouth and pulling it. But resistance was impossible. One evening, the matron called me to her house, told me to remove my clothes and lie down, legs open. At nine years, I could not muster the courage to object. I did as she said. She then started pulling me. With every pull, I felt like she was tearing me. I wanted to cry. But I knew better than to show her that what she was doing was painful and uncomfortable. I just turned and faced the wall. When I got up and dressed, she told me to continue every day doing what she had just done.

Walking back to my dormitory, I felt like someone was holding a fire in my knickers. I was burning. I jumped into bed and cried myself to sleep.

The next morning, I could barely wash my privates; it felt like I was washing with chili. I limped back to the dormitory, and spent the day in discomfort. I was not alone. Some other girls also walked with a limp like me. Obviously, they had been "helped" by the senior woman too.

I still couldn't imagine putting myself through such pain again. But the senior woman warned that she would check every girl one by one to see how far we had progressed, and she promised to punish those who had not made progress. Girls who refused, she said, would be taken to the trading center and undressed. Then, millet grain would be poured into their vaginas, and the strongest rooster would be brought to eat the millet. This woman had never lied when she threatened to punish us. So I complied, as did every other girl who had tried to avoid pulling. The mere thought of standing naked in front of people, let alone having a bird pecking at our privates, scared us so much we would do anything she instructed.

It wasn't until a few years later that I finally learned why I was made to pull. The girls in my high school said that elongating the labia was meant to help our future husbands enjoy sex. The elongated labia are believed to help keep the vagina warm and enhance foreplay. Pulled labia, it is said, are like a nice gate in front of a mansion. They symbolize warm reception, give the visitor pleasant visual nutrition, and create an impression that the host cordially welcomes her guests. It is said that making love to a woman who hasn't pulled is like diving into the Grand Canyon – the only fun is inside.

So, it seems, a woman's life of service begins with reshaping her body.

By the time I met Ssenga Hamidah, newer, "modern" influences had blended with my traditional lessons about womanhood. While I had pulled and learned how to kneel for men, I also had been to university, ended my virginity and had all my questions about sex answered. I also had watched South American telenovelas, which showed men looking intensely into the eyes of women and vowing undying love (when they weren't fighting off competition from other men, that is). I had seen western movies that depicted women being as casual about sex as men. I had watched music videos that featured women gyrating in skimpy clothes, flaunting sexuality and skin. And like many of my peers, I had fed on American soap operas, which depicted married women shouting at their husbands to cook, clean and otherwise divide domestic chores.

Meanwhile, I got a job, and started earning enough to support myself and live an independent life. I enjoyed my freedom to ponder diverse role models without committing myself to any single one.

But my friend's bridal shower led me to confront long-standing issues. Weddings are times for tradition – a fact my friends and I acknowledged by inviting the ssenga to the shower. This woman who talked about the importance of kneeling and who writhed on the floor in simulated sex perplexed me. Even as I joined in scoffing at her, I felt uncomfortable.

Like my friends, I found much of the ssenga's teaching absurd. I refuse to accept that my duty would be merely to keep my man happy at all times and at all cost. I could not understand why I would have to kneel and do all the work around the house when I, too, would bring home money that supports the family. I could not accept that I shouldn't tell my future husband what I need in bed. How could it be that women were always supposed to be givers and never receivers?

And yet, Ssenga Hamidah couldn't be easily dismissed. She was taking us through lessons passed down from our ancestors for many generations. We knew that ssengas still teach these lessons to our country's many simple village girls – girls who vastly outnumber us city sophisticates. Should we take our emancipated talk and shove it down their throats? Could the old ways really be without any value?

As I thought about it, I worried that maybe we modern Ugandan women were rebelling on the basis of a superficial impression we have of western values – an impression that we gather from soap operas and movies, and assume to be superior to our own society's old ways. I wasn't even sure these popular images matched the reality in the west, let alone Ugandan values. When I visited America for the first time in 2009, I was surprised to discover that women – even Rihanna – do not prance down the streets half naked. I also knew that other cultures exalt values similar to the ones I had been taught. In Asia, men and women both bow in respect when greeting each other. As for pulling, I understand that some whites have vaginal rings. And while African women may wear beads around their waists, Arabs wear chains around their bellies to bed. Are Africans wearing beads really any different from western women who wear silky lingerie to bed?

Although we laughed at her, Ssenga Hamidah wasn't exactly an obsolete cultural relic. She has clients from all over the world – from America, Asia and the Arab world – who want to have their labia elongated (she charges $110 for a three-week treatment). And western men come to see what pulled labia look and feel like.

How could I reconcile the many thoughts swirling around in my mind? I certainly didn't want to become an unthinking defender of old ways, but I didn't want to be a knee-jerk "modern" woman in the western mould either. I realized that there is a deeper meaning and value to traditional culture that transcends specific prescriptions about pulling, kneeling or washing off your man after having sex. But I was uncertain how to adapt these values to modern times.

I did know this: Society still needs many of the values ssengas teach – like modesty and the virtue of putting others ahead of ourselves. We all would be better off if everyone believed that caring for others and upholding the peace, comfort, pleasure and stability of family and society are more important than getting ahead individually.

Of course, these values were just part of the traditional contract. The other part is that men have their exalted positions because they have great responsibilities – to provide for others, to keep the peace, and to uphold laws and moral values. Sadly, as women rebel against traditional culture, the male part of traditional values also is suffering. Men have concocted their own self-serving mix of old and new. They happily embrace emancipation when it serves them – wanting, for instance, to divide bills right down the middle or to partake of liberated women's commitment-free love – but they still expect their wives to kneel, cook, clean and wait at home in warm beds with beads around their waists and terry cloths in hand.

What's the solution?

I'm still working on it. But I am not going to let culture and tradition go down the drain.

Did I pull? Yes. And if you think it will improve your sex life, you should too.

Will I wash my man after sex? Maybe, but I would expect him to wash me too. Or maybe we should take a shower together.

Will I continue to be humble and show my man respect? Yes, but I want a man who commands respect without asking for it – one who is responsible and strong, who acknowledges my contribution, and who works with me to raise a good family and be part of a good society.

Will I kneel before my man? It depends on where I am: I certainly will kneel in front of relatives and elders for culture's sake. I have no problem with presenting myself as a modest, self-sacrificing person and following a small ritual that honors the ideals that men are supposed to represent. But in private? There, my man better be ready to kneel for me too.

Gods and Ghosts

By Lydia Namubiru

I am standing on a softly moon-lit beach in Zanzibar. At my feet lies a smooth carpet of softly glowing sand, erased of all features by the relentless waves of the Indian Ocean. A full moon has just risen, laying a sparkling path from the horizon to my feet. This is the kind of night to take the hand of the one you love and walk down the beach talking about everything from the existential to the trite. But I will be doing no such thing.

The shiver going down my spine isn't from the romance in the air. It is fear – fear of the invisible, vast sea a few meters away. Silent, dark and unknown, the night ocean is a perfect setting for the demons of my ancestors' time. I know it's absurd, but I can picture a dark, bony fiend floating somewhere in the dark. What if it were to dislike my loitering on its territory? It could extinguish me in a flash. Even when I dismiss this imaginary demon as perhaps a little melodramatic, I still shudder at the thought of mysterious forces out there. So I quickly turn back towards the world of people and light.

I am a grown, educated and rational woman. Perhaps I should get beyond childish fears of imaginary demons. But, alas, the things you learn as a child are hard to unlearn.

I first encountered the mysterious unknown of the African spiritual life when I was about eight years old. The village's only Muslim patriarch, Mukiibi Abdul, was very sick – dying, they said. So of course, every child in the village ran to his homestead to see how a person dies. But almost as soon as we got there we heard something that drove us away. The cause of Mukiibi's illness reportedly had been pinpointed: A malevolent neighbor had set demons upon him. By the time we arrived, an exorcist had already reached the ailing man's house to expel the evil spirits.

The evil neighbor happened to be a slightly odd-looking man with pronounced bow legs, a fact that might explain why he had earned labels such as "wizard," "cannibal" and "night fiend." At the time, I was too young to have much humor or to see through these labels. I completely believed that this man was everything scary that people said and more. So when I heard that his demons were within Mukiibi's house, I ran right out of the invaded compound and across the village path that skirted it, choosing to witness the exorcism or possible death of a man from a safe distance.

Soon the exorcism was underway. I knew this when I saw Mukiibi's 12-year-old daughter come out of the house. Delicately and fearfully, she stepped into the compound murmuring what appeared to be a repetitive chant. With one hand angled slightly behind the rest of her body, she moved her fingers in an almost frantic come-hither way, as if to beckon a follower to keep pace with her. But nobody could be seen following her, at least not with the naked eye. In a few trips, she led the demons away from her father's property, dumping them just a few meters into the trou-ble-making neighbor's farm. Mukiibi survived.

Uganda is a potent mix of religiosity and spirituality. Nominally, 80% of Ugandans are Christian, and most of the rest have been instructed in Islam or some other imported belief system. We even have people whose religion is Judaism. Behind these foreign religions lie our traditional African beliefs and practices. There are no standards for balancing our imported faiths with our ancestral ones, but most people, whether they acknowledge it or not, straddle the fence. It is not unusual to find a father who attempts to secure his children a place in heaven by baptizing them Christian, but who turns to the traditional spirits to secure his wealth by occasionally sacrificing a cock or goat in the presence of a spiritual medium.

Muslims like Mukiibi aren't rare either. A story is told (in whispers of course) that Mukiibi once tortured his sister in hopes of causing her a miscarriage because she had conceived with a Christian man. Yet, when his life was on the line, Mukiibi didn't turn to his Islamic faith for redemption – at least not exclusively.

Growing up, I observed and absorbed this fluidity in spirituality without opinion or question. In fact, I enjoyed it. I especially enjoyed a time when my distant cousin, Kizito, joined the New Apostolic Church. He had come upon white missionaries who were looking to spread their new faith. In very short order, he accepted their religion and was baptized, ordained as a priest and sent to his own village to convert others. Of course, we already had our own religions – faiths we had ostensibly been born into. I was Catholic because my father was. My grandmother and the rest of the family I lived with were Anglican Protestants. The neighbors to the East were Catholic. Mukiibi and his family to the northeast were Muslims. Kizito was an Anglican before his conversion.

When Kizito came to the village to introduce the new religion, he was quite honest with the adults. He didn't expect them to quit their religions. He just wanted them to attend his services as well. That suited nearly everyone. They could support his new career without abandoning their faiths. So each Sunday, after going to our own churches, we all gathered for Kizito's services. The Muslim Mukiibi let us use his compound, and his sons served as ushers. But this was no problem. So in these unusual circumstances and that unlikely place, Kizito solemnly took us through the New Apostolic service.

In my childish estimation, Kizito's rites beat the proper ones by far. For one, children didn't have to sit stiffly through the whole ordeal; instead, we perched ourselves in trees for the entire service, only coming down briefly to take Holy Communion. And that was the cookie: Kizito served Holy Communion to all and sundry. You didn't have to study catechism or know what to say when he held that little white bread before you! Only if you have grown up Catholic can you appreciate what a break that was.

Usually our ecumenical approach didn't bother the adults, but every now and then lines would be drawn to keep one realm of spirituality separate from another. For instance, when Kizito brought "holy water" to baptize the congregation one day, the adults allowed him to baptize the children but refused to get baptized themselves. Apparently, that would have been crossing the line into blasphemy.

Ironically, such lines were drawn most boldly and frequently to exclude African traditional religion from contemporary spiritual practice. As a child, the only times I ever heard about the

African spiritual practices was during health crises like Mukiibi's. Two episodes involving my own family stick with me especially clearly.

One involves the family of a man who married my mother's cousin. In a seemingly pathological search for power (or at least in a bid to terrorize neighbors), her brother-in-law is said to have bought demons to visit disease and death upon people who crossed him. Apparently, the demons needed more blood than he had enemies, so they turned on his immediate and extended family. An aunt of mine lost at least four children in a short span of time during their pre-teens, and another became crippled. The demons brought by their power-hungry uncle were blamed for all the deaths. With each burial, tales of the bizarre came flying off the tongues of the mourners, all attributed to that man: An earthquake struck during one, a large serpent emerged from a grave during another, and thunder and a heavenly body landed on the roof in the next.

Another tale was told by my mum, a university graduate and staunch Christian. Once when she was in teachers-training college, a friend of hers became very ill. The family called a healer, who consulted spirits. He divined that a certain woman whom the boy's father had ditched after a short affair had sent demons hidden in animal horns to attack him. The healer said the demons were buried in the family's banana plantation. With my mother holding a lamp for him, he walked through the plantation at night, tapping the ground. At intervals, my mother reports, little horns jumped out of certain spots and rolled on the ground. The healer would follow them and tap them with his stick to stop their movement. My mother said he collected a tidy number of horns. That very night, the boy's swelling started to come down, and the next day he regained his speech.

I know how ridiculous and childish these stories sound, but more than two billion Christians and Jews believe that a serpent talked to Eve. So cut me some slack!

Like most Ugandans, I sit on the fence between different spiritual worlds. But unlike most Ugandans I balance degrees of *disbelief* rather than belief. Exposed to many organized religions and angered at some for their inglorious roles in my people's history (Christianity came with colonialism and Islam with the slave trade), I pledge allegiance to none. At the same time, I steer clear of African traditional beliefs, having for many years been fed scary notions regarding them. Yet once when I was laid on a surgical table, I gave my life to Christ, just in case. When my daughter was six weeks old, I shaved her head clean on the religious recommendation of my Muslim roommate. Then there is my nightly fear of big water bodies, forests and graveyards. While in my rational, waking hours I don't believe that demons exist, nothing would induce me to enter the shrine of a traditional diviner.

My lack of religious affiliation makes me unusual. In Uganda, one's religion is almost as important as his clan, and one who does not belong to an organized religion risks being seen either as an outcast or a rebel. But I fell through the cracks. I was born of an Anglican mother and a Roman Catholic father. My parents separated when I was very young. I was raised by my maternal grandmother for six years, and after that by my mother. You might think the Anglican influence would be greater, but Uganda is a patrilineal culture, so I was deemed a Catholic even though I had no relationship with my father. When my grandmother and her family went to Church on Sundays, they sent me to join a neighboring Catholic family to worship in their church. Later, when I went to live with my mother, she gave me some religious instruction, telling me bible stories. But she, too, honored tradition and found someone to take me to a Catholic church on Sundays. When I was 13, she even sent me to a boarding school run by Catholic nuns. But since most children were fully introduced to their religion by age 13, the nuns did not have an active program for introducing students to Catholicism. Instead, they led us through routines like rosary recitals, mass, penance sessions and personal prayers. These shallow rituals and my lack of focused familial grounding in religion left me less than committed spiritually.

My commitment to a path of non-belief was confirmed when I discovered as a teenager that I could use my lack of religion as a popularity stunt. Since everyone else was tied to a religion and I was not, I was unique – and therefore "totally cool." Or so I reasoned. But then the adult world drew me into a different kind of calculation. My mother finally came clean and told me that I had never been baptized. Her family considered baptism a father's responsibility, but my father was absent, so nobody had taken up the duty. This might seem irrelevant since I was a budding atheist, but my mother's revelation offered me an irresistible opportunity for rebellion: I could try to make her feel guilty for failing to have me baptized, while asserting my feminism by rejecting her suggestion that I go to my father now to get the job done. So I defiantly went to a different church and organized my own baptism. That's how I came to be dipped into a pool of water at the Kampala Pentecostal Church, in the process accepting Jesus as my personal savior.

I tried for a few years to make good on my promise to live a devout life, but eventually I grew bored. Time moved on. In college, I learned to intellectualize about religion, seeing it, as an anthropologist might, as a means of social control. Eventually, education softened my hard edges, and I came to recognize that religion can be, for some, a source of solace in a cruel world. But I saw little need for it myself. By chance, my best friends at the time were Muslim. Yet as much as I loved them, I couldn't accept their ritualistic worship, perhaps because Christianity had bred in me a fear of ritualism and its close association with traditional African religion, which has been demonized to all of us.

So here I am – a non-practicing pagan. Why pagan? That's the other half of this story.

Before the imported religions entered the African picture, my forebears believed in a three-tier spiritual world. At the top was a supreme God known as Katonda, or "Creator." Very little was known about Him. Although special shrines were dedicated to him, people did not routinely consult Him, and He was not expected to intervene in human affairs.

Below Katonda, about two dozen autonomous spirits formed the focal point of the organized religious activities of the tribe. Each spirit governed a different aspect of human life – hunting, war, fertility, earthquakes, physical handicaps and so on. Some said spirits were like Roman Catholic saints – humans of exceptional qualities who were venerated upon their deaths. Others stressed that their powers were supernatural. Kibuuka, the war spirit, is said to have been an exceptional soldier in his lifetime, for instance. He would fly like a bird over the battlefield and rain arrows down on enemy soldiers. Upon his death, he became the war spirit; before any military campaign, the tribe would consult him and offer sacrifices in return for his advice and intercession. Spirits had shrines, and could be reached through human beings, or mediums, but they wouldn't intercede on behalf of a supplicant until their own demands, communicated through the medium, were satisfied. Often, spirits asked for things like fattened he-goats or white cocks. When these were presented, they would promise to deal with people's concerns. The seekers then would leave, confident that their prayers would be answered.

At the lowest tier of the spiritual hierarchy were ghosts. Most immediate to human beings, they were spirits of departed ancestors, but also included special spirits who lived in nearby forests, hills or streams. Every homestead had a shrine where the family spirits lived. Usually these were just baskets into which a few coffee beans or cowrie shells were regularly thrown, but some families set aside entire huts as shrines. Family spirits were mostly benevolent, although a few made outrageous demands and acted viciously when displeased. Rituals to these family spirits did not need any assistance from mediums.

The spirits who dwelled in village hills, forests or streams usually were unfriendly, but the only duty people owed them was not to displease them. Most of these spirits were satisfied simply by being avoided; a spirit in the form of a beautiful woman might bathe in a local stream each day at noon, for instance, so villagers could never set foot in the stream any time near midday lest she strike them dead or haunt them at night for invading her privacy. Some spirits would ask for more, though. A python spirit might threaten to eat livestock or even children unless people left eggs at the entrance to the cave where it lived, for instance.

Parallel to that spiritual world was another one that was believed to be evil. This was – and still is – the realm where witch doctors, both male and female, practice. They supposedly are of two types: those who possess and dispatch evil spirits and those who heal people afflicted by the evil spirits. Most claim to perform both tasks. I can neither prove nor disprove their powers or the actual existence of their world.

Presumably, Mukiibi's neighbor and my aunt's brother-in-law visited the evil side of the divide to get their purported demons. Mukiibi's neighbor was said to keep demons in a hut behind his house, and hold consultations with people who wanted to hire them to terrorize or kill their enemies. If you annoyed him, he would send them after you, and they would make you sick or even kill you. It also was said that at night, he would be possessed by a cannibal demon; he then would undress and run around the village, dig up graves and take home the bodies to be eaten by his family. His family was largely isolated by the other villagers. Today, I wonder whether they were stigmatized because they were pronouncedly bowlegged. But back then, when I was about four years old, the mere mention of his name would send me scampering into the house. To date, fear is my first reaction to people who practice African religion.

When I was 12, one of the girls in my dormitory at school said that she had been visited by the spirit of her deceased grandmother. Apparently the spirit continued to visit her, and with each new visit it made a fresh demand. The girl said the spirit did not want any of us to sleep on the lowest deck of our double-decker beds. So we shared beds with those on the upper bunks. With time, the girl relayed more minutes of her meetings with the grandma spirit, and we got increasingly scared. One night, shortly after we had switched off the lights, I heard a door creaking as if it were being forced off its hinges. Then I heard the sound of it being thrown violently against the wall, and a huge gush of wind burst into the room. "You are welcome, *Jjaja* (grandpa/grandma)," the girl said. They had a long talk (we heard only the girl's side). Then, another gush of wind blew and I heard the sound of a door slamming. I swear that I did not imagine this.

When I was in the Catholic school, we used to have retreats that ended with a specially anointed priest conducting a healing mass. I saw some bizarre things as the priest supposedly expelled demons of different origins out of students. Once, I remember a little girl who jumped around like a monkey at a mere touch by the priest. According to the priest, her family had offered her to the family spirit in exchange for their conversion to Christianity. So the family ghosts resided in her!

Childish as such tales may sound, I, like many Ugandans, cannot completely let go of them. It is easy for me today to scoff at supernatural claims made by Christians, Muslims or other members of organized religions. But in spite of my best, rational efforts, I cannot so easily dismiss these stories from my own homeland. So I try not to scratch beneath the surface of African religion.

Today, I am firmly ensconced on the fence between religious traditions. There is much I admire about imported religion. I think the New Testament is an excellent guide to living a good human life, and I love Jesus' teachings. But to me, tales that Jesus was the son of God who rose from the dead and ascended into heaven diminish the fact that he was a truly phenomenal and timeless human being. The preachers (and imams) have demystified life. They tell us to forget whatever unanswered questions we may still have. I cannot abide that.

I find much of my ancestral religion interesting and appealing too. Its closeness to nature. The fact that it doesn't try to answer the most unanswerable questions, such as the nature of the Creator. The way it recognizes important social and psychological truths, such as the human desire to make the lives and wisdom of loved ones count beyond their natural time on earth. Of course, I am aware of the evil often associated with traditional religion – incidents of human sacrifice, for instance. But these, I believe, are the work of cults veiled as traditionalism. Every religion has spurred evil imitations. Traditionalism cannot be judged by the actions of psychopaths who kill people in some twisted form of worship any more than Islam can be judged by Bin Laden extremism, or the murder-suicides of the Order of the Solar Temple in Switzerland or the Rev. Jim Jones in Guyana. I regret, however, that traditional religion offers no guidance on how to live a moral life. And I wonder what knowledge or help it might have offered in the olden days that I will never know because the imported religions relegated it to people's backyards and private thoughts.

> *I recently stood on another sandy ocean beach in the moonlight. Again, the pale light and soft thunder of the waves created a dreamlike aura. Again, the dark, formless ocean stretched, still and mysterious, beyond my vision. This time I was less afraid.*

"He Will Kill Me"

By Peace Twine

The tears were still flowing when my mother voiced her frightful lament. I had just told her I was pregnant. I was 19 years old. While the legal age for marriage In Uganda is 18, I was unmarried – a situation sure to bring shame and ridicule – or maybe, as my mother's words suggested, something even worse to me and my family. The "he" in her frightful lament, "He will kill me," was my father.

At the time – the early 1970s – sex was taboo. It was rarely discussed either within families or in the mass media. Like me, many girls were ignorant of what exactly sex was and under what circumstances it took place. But Satan is ready to attack at any opportunity. One night, I had stayed out with friends until it was too late to go back to our boarding school, so we spent the night drinking and dancing. This made me vulnerable, and I succumbed to the advances of a boy who had tried to befriend me for more than a year.

I kept my condition a secret for seven months. I sat for final examinations at my secondary school when I was three months pregnant. I talked to no one. When my funny moods and strange new appetites could no longer be ignored, I relied on my biology text books to learn what was happening to me. I kept myself busy, and tried to ignore the changes that were taking place in my small body. By the time I talked with my mother, I had a temporary job teaching at a secondary school while awaiting my examination results. I had been traveling home nearly every weekend, often bringing with me things for the family and my siblings. My parents were proud of me. Life was good. But I was in denial.

My world came crashing down around me after my mother heard a rumor in our village that I was pregnant. She waited until I came home the next weekend. She welcomed me as usual when I arrived, but the next morning, when I went to the garden with her, she finally asked if the story was true. I did not know what to say. I started crying. My mother also broke down. She blamed herself more than she blamed me, and bemoaned the fact she had not been more observant. She was ashamed to think she was the last person in the village to know about my situation. But more than that, she worried about what my father would do.

I never believed for a moment that my pregnancy was a sin. It was an accident. I did not believe it was grave enough to get someone killed. I wondered why my mother would be killed because of my accident, which, after all, was not hurting anyone. Later, my mother told me she was worried not just for herself. She feared that I could be taken to Kisiizi, where in the past unknown numbers of unwed pregnant girls had been thrown over a steep cliff by their brothers. No one knew whether the girls died in mid-air because of fright, on the way down when they hit rocks, or when they reached the water in the valley and drowned. While the girls paid the ultimate price, their families suffered too. The fact that a daughter would be killed and would not have a grave in the homestead was punishment for the whole family. By the time I became pregnant, the practice had nearly stopped – reportedly after one girl pulled her brother over the cliff with her – but some families still banished unmarried pregnant daughters and their mothers. And even if my mother and I faced a less horrible fate, her pain was punishment enough.

I kept thinking of her words as I grew up. I realized that women die many times in life. They die when something happens to them or their families that is outside what is culturally accepted. That is the lasting meaning of the phrase, "He will kill me."

My mother's tears – and especially her fear about my father – woke me to the gravity of my predicament. When we went home from the garden that day, we acted as if nothing had happened, but in fact everything had changed. I felt guilty for causing problems for my mother, and I did not want to be near my father. If he could kill my mother, what would he do to me? My mother asked me not to come back home in my condition. What was I to do, and where would I go?

The next morning, my father escorted me to the bus. He acted normal and seemed friendly, but he was quiet. I could not tell if he knew my secret. I was afraid of him. Based on what my mother had said, I did not take him as a loving and understanding father, but as a judge who would condemn and punish me. If I had remembered the biblical teachings that our heavenly Father is kind and just when we confess our sins, maybe I would have talked to my father openly about my predicament. But I did not have the biblical knowledge to apply to my earthly experience, and my mother's words echoed in my mind. "He will kill me."

Only later did I learn that my father had noticed my pregnancy long before my mother did, but was watching to see what she would do. When I look back, I realize that he would have loved to help or at least advise me, but was too shy to talk to me about my condition.

Education saved me. Because of it, I had a job, an income and a house where I could take refuge. The same father who frightened me gets a good share of the credit for giving me education.

Formal education was introduced in Uganda in colonial times. Closely linked to religion, it brought many new beliefs and ways of living. But it divided many families too. The educated and uneducated took different paths. Family relations were weakened, while new networks were formed. My father, Kalekyezi, and his elder brother, Festo, illustrated the divide.

Kalekyezi was brought up by a cousin who had gone to school. He helped with housework and gardening, and was given education. Festo stayed with their mother, and did not get education. My father was able to meet and marry my mother, who thanks to missionaries also had been sent to school and had become a school teacher. My uncle was given an illiterate girl for a wife.

I grew up in a middle class, Christian family. My parents had 10 children. I learned to claim middle-class status to avoid quarrels with my siblings who often accused me of undermining the family's status whenever I said I grew up in a poor family. But I gradually appreciated that my family really was wealthy. Our wealth was not in cattle or cash, though. It was in knowledge and information received from our parents, the education system and the radio (I did not watch television until the mid-1980s).

Festo and his wife had a low opinion of education. He never realized what he missed in life by not being educated. So he never encouraged his children to complete their own educations. It was not a matter of money. In the colonial and post-independence times, there were many well-wishers who would send young boys and girls to school. But the will to work hard in the community and in class was required, and those who had never been educated often lacked it.

Conflicts over the importance of education could be pretty intense, as I learned at 17, when my uncle urged my father to take me out of school rather than let me return for the final two years of my secondary education. Girls from families like Festo's did not even step into a classroom. Their parents were scared of sending them to school lest they would fail to get married or, once away from their parents' watchful eyes, get pregnant outside marriage.

One night, Festo got drunk to gain courage to confront my father. "What is this that I hear, Kalekyezi?' he asked. "The girl is going away again to school?"

"She passed her examinations and is going back," Kalekyezi responded proudly. "We are happy."

"You must be out of your mind or stupid to send her back! Don't you realize she is growing too old? Why don't you get her married?" Festo demanded.

"It is never too late to get married…"

"If our father were alive, you wouldn't be taking this issue lightly. I know you don't respect me and my opinion because I didn't go to school – even though I am your elder brother!" Festo now was shouting. Invoking his father, who was long gone, showed that this was serious.

"This will be for only two years," Kalekyezi tried to explain. "And she can get married after her education."

"Two years? Don't you want us to get cows in this compound?" Festo sounded shocked as he raised the issue of bride price, the obligation that grooms' families must pay brides' families to take in their daughters. "Or don't you care for cows anymore because you are a teacher? Remember, Peace is as much my daughter as she is yours, and the clan should also have a say in the matter."

"Don't threaten me with the clan," Kalekyezi said, trying to end the fight.

Festo got up angrily, waving his walking stick at his brother. "You think I am drunk, and don't know what I am saying? I will care about my girls, the ones I have brought into this world, and I want to assure you that they will do the right thing. They will get married, all of them, before yours. That is what you want?"

Festo walked home without waiting for an answer. He was angry and defeated. Time would tell which of the two men was right. I would be the test case. But it was not clear at first which brother could claim vindication. I may have gone on to get an education, but my parents, the education system and the media of that time all failed to keep me from having a child before I was married.

The bus ride back to my place of work after the fateful weekend when I told my mother I was pregnant was the longest trip I had ever made. With a mother who was frightened and did not want to see me again and a father who was as distant as a heavenly Father when one has sinned, I seemed to be on an endless journey with no destination. I knew I was on my own.

After many days of wondering, I finally decided to write to a maternal aunt. I was buying time. But time was not on my side. The fetus in me was growing. No other solutions appeared, and when my aunt invited me to her home in Kampala during the school holidays, I went. The night I reached Kampala, I failed to sleep. I kept turning, rising to go to the toilet at frequent intervals. My grandmother, who was also at my auntie's home, said I was in labor! God's way of doing things is not our way. There I was, with no arrangement for the baby, no clothes, nothing. If it was today, in the 21st century, I would have been in great trouble and danger.

When I got to the hospital, the nurses prepared me for delivery. Luckily, I had some money to buy baby clothes from women who sell them in maternity wards. That would not have been the case if I did not have a job. I was more or less financially independent due to my academic status. I gave birth to a baby girl.

I have never been more confused than I was during the days I was in hospital with my baby. I had been told not to go back home pregnant, but could I go with a baby? Would I go back to school? Would I still have a place to teach now that I had to take care of myself and a little girl? Discharged from hospital two days after I gave birth, I picked up my baby and the few things I had bought for her, and got into a vehicle that took us some twelve kilometers from Kampala to another auntie's home. She had more room in her house and was staying alone, so I could keep her company. I was so lucky to have people to take care of me at my time of confusion. It was because my aunties were educated, working and so financially independent that they were able to help me.

While my mother's family cared for me and made my problem their problem, they did not completely forgive me. They reminded me how I had brought problems to my mother. They had written to her that I had given birth, but they could not imagine what my father would say.

One day, Aunt Juliet came with good news. "You are lucky. You passed the advanced level examinations, and can join university," she said. But echoing my mother's earlier statement, she added: "Otherwise, your father would have killed you."

Once again, education saved me. Unlike other new entrants to university, I had to think of who was to take care of my baby when I went to university. But I got a job as an English teacher in the village primary school for the months before university started. The salary enabled me to pay a baby sitter and buy necessities.

My mother came to see me three months after my daughter was born. She told me my father was happy that I was going to complete my education, and that he planned to confront the baby's father. She invited me to take the baby home, and offered to look after her as I went to university. I was so happy to be accepted back by my family.

I did not disappoint my parents again. I completed my education and got married. My uncles' girls and boys were all married by then. My uncle must have realized too late that his idea of early marriage was not the best way to get rich. His family remained subsistence peasants.

I got married at 28 years, and became a mother again to four children – two boys and two girls. I am now a grandmother to seven children.

My first pregnancy taught me many things. It showed me that men have a special place in the lives of the children they bring into the world. Society isolates men from children in the false belief that bringing up children is the role of women alone, not men. We still tend to blame a mother when something goes wrong with the children, while giving men credit when something good happens. Society should not deny either parent a place in the lives of children as they grow up.

I also learned the importance of communication. Better communication might have taught me how to avoid pregnancy in the first place, and it would have saved my family much pain. If my mother had discussed my dilemma with my father, she would not have shed tears after realizing I was pregnant. And if my father had been able to talk with her and me, he would have been able to play the protective role he wanted to play – the same strong role he played when he sheltered me from uncles who wanted me married rather than educated.

I married a man who was as liberal as my father, and my children did not fear discussing issues with us. Communication keeps us together. There are no "he will kill me" fears in my family. At the same time, HIV/AIDS has led to much more candor in the media about sex. My children have not made the same mistake I did.

But sometimes I wonder if things have improved. Today's parents are busy with survival and selfish pursuits. They leave children to the house help and schools. In some cases, day-care centers take in children who are only a few months old, and some schools admit children as young as three.

Technology has improved communication, but it has hurt it too. Old cultural practices once isolated men from women and children, but modern technology isolates the young from the old. Children talk to parents while watching television or using their phones. Parents rely on the mass media to instruct their children, but it is not as effective as old-fashioned, face-to-face communication. Ironically, some of the best opportunities for communication today come when technology fails. In my family, nights without electricity and television give us some of our best opportunities to talk. But we cannot rely solely on technological failure, so we also have regular family Sunday lunches.

More people are learning the value of education. While Festo's children were never educated, they are sending their children to school. It is not easy, though. Education has become more expensive in the 21st century, and less beneficial in the job market if one does not go to the right schools. And while education has helped us, it continues to divide us too. There is nothing more painful today than going to a village and finding no one to talk to because everyone shies away, thinking you are more educated than they are.

Wife of the Enemy

By Peace Twine

It began with a knock on the door.

I was in my room at the university. My friend, Hope, had just come in, as she often did after lectures, to drop off her books and change into comfortable walking shoes so we could go to the market to buy food for supper after the day's work.

"Come in. The door is open," we said in unison to the unknown visitor rapping on the door. We were in a happy mood, and did not even turn our heads to see who was calling.

Though decades apart in age, Hope and I were close friends. She was middle aged. After an early pregnancy forced her to drop out of school, she married and raised five children. But she eventually enrolled in a teacher-training college, earned her diploma and started a career as a teacher. When her husband died in a car accident, she persevered, earning a second degree and landing a teaching position at the university while pursuing a master's degree in education.

My path had been much easier – straight from high school to university. I held an assistant teaching position, and was doing research for my own master's degree. But like Hope, I also had a child I was raising alone. That, and the fact we both stayed in Uganda to care for our dependents rather than travel to another country for our education, may help explain our common bond.

The door opened, and in walked a man neither of us knew. "Who stays in this room?" he demanded. Through the open door behind him, I could see another man waiting outside.

I told him it was my room, and asked whom he was seeking. "I am from Internal Affairs. We got a report that you had a visitor who we are interested in. Can you come with us?" He eyed Hope standing beside me, and added: "Who is this one? You can also come along."

Hope started to ask something, but the man cut her off. "Ladies, please do not waste our time. Get up, and let us go."

Hope and I both glanced at our watches. Perhaps if we hurried, we could clear matters up and still get to the market as we planned. I turned to get our bags, but the man barked, "You do not need bags, so do not waste time." He stepped out the door to stand beside the other man who had stayed there.

I only had time to pick up a small purse, and give Hope a pair of flat shoes she could wear instead of high heels. "I hope we will come back quickly because I do not remember any visitor coming to my room recently," I said as I locked the door.

Outside, we casually greeted neighbors. The two men walked closely behind us, directing us to a Land Rover. We climbed in the rear seat, pleased with the thought that it could take us to our destination quickly so we could then get to the market. "Try to remember who came to visit you," Hope joked. "At least I know it is not me because I come every day."

With the two men sitting quietly in the front seat, we headed toward town. We were still unconcerned. In fact, we felt privileged to be in a car, since other days we would be among the people we now watched walking in the hot afternoon sun and dust. We did not know where we were going, and we knew little about the Ministry of Internal Affairs, but we trusted the government. Led by Milton Obote, it had replaced the notorious military government of Idi Amin. It was no secret that when the country attempted to restore multi-party democracy a year before, some people were disgruntled, complaining of vote rigging. But I had never participated in voting because I did not understand the process. And although a rebel group called the National Resistance Army was mobilizing and fighting in the central part of the country, I considered it my responsibility to work with the government to keep the peace our country was enjoying.

Hope and I were too busy, too focused on our studies, and too eager for degrees that would help us care for ourselves and our families to be interested in politics.

Before long, the vehicle stopped at what we learned was the Central Police Station. We had never even known about it before, but we remained unconcerned. Police stations were built for wrong-doers and thieves, we thought, as the men ordered us to follow them inside, told us to sit on a bench in the reception area and walked away without saying anything.

There we sat. As afternoon turned to evening, Hope asked if we had been forgotten. We got up to ask, but a policeman at the desk shouted, "Where do you think you are going? Sit down. You are not going anywhere."

Three more hours passed. It was now dark outside. Few people came into the reception area. Eventually, nobody was left except us, one man seated nearby, and the policeman who watched us.

Another policeman entered. The two murmured about us, and we heard the first guard speculate that we had been brought in for "safe custody." We had never heard the term, and although we were now tired and frustrated, we were not alarmed. But then we heard the incoming policeman tell the other, "You should take them inside before you leave because it is getting late. I do not think they will be taken tonight."

I lost my temper. "This is not happening. Why? How can you people be so heartless?" I shouted at the first policeman, who had picked up a bunch of keys and was moving toward us. I wanted to explain that this all was a big mistake, but I was given no chance.

"What do you mean we are heartless?" the policeman said. "Are we the ones who brought you here? Our duty is to make sure we hand you over to the people who brought you to us. Now get up and let us go this way."

At that, we were led inside and then through a corridor that ended in a stairway going down. We descended, and found ourselves at the beginning of another corridor. From down this hallway, we heard voices. It finally dawned on me that I wasn't simply being held for questioning. I wasn't a suspect. I was a prisoner.

The policeman in front of us was walking fast, but he kept looking back to make sure we were following. We reached a metallic door with bars, and there we saw the source of the voices we had heard: We saw men looking at us from behind the bars. Many others were seated behind them farther inside. They had no shirts and only shorts or trousers.

Hope held my arm as we followed the policeman past the men's cell as quickly as we could. We were scared, fearing even to look at the locked-up men. All we knew of prisoners is that they were cruel and dishonest. Compared to them, the policeman's presence actually seemed comforting.

Then we reached the women's cell. The policeman stopped and opened an outer, metallic door. Through the bars of a second door, we could see women of all ages, sizes and complexions. They all looked unclean, with untidy hair. Some sat on the cement floor, some stood. A few lay down. Lucky ones had mats or pieces of cloth. Others had nothing but the bare floor beneath them. There was a strong stench of urine and sweat.

"Enter," the policeman said, holding open the second door. We entered slowly, carefully and fearfully. The door closed as soon as we were inside. "Let us hope you will have someone to get you out tomorrow."

The women surrounded us and stared. I clung to Hope, and felt tears falling.

Mwe! Babaretedeki? "Why have you been brought here?" a short, stout woman asked as she moved close.

"We do not know," Hope and I answered simultaneously.

"Do not tell us a lie," shouted an elderly, brown woman squatting in the corner. You must have done something. Do not try to be clever."

"Welcome to prison," another yelled mockingly. "That is what we all said the first time we were arrested."

"Do not cry. You will get used to this," said another in a quieter tone.

Confused and scared, we edged toward a small open space at the end of the room. Only when we got there did we realize it was next to the toilet bucket. When we sat, the smell of human waste was overpowering. But all we could do was look down to disguise the fear and tears in our eyes as we were besieged with more questions.

"Have you just been arrested?"

"How come you have your shoes on?"

"They could be spies. Better be careful, my friend."

"Even if you are spies, you should be good so that we can get you better space away from our toilet." This last comment provoked laughter from everyone except from us. By now we were sobbing openly.

"We asked you, why were you arrested?" the stout woman asked slowly but with emphasis, as if she was warning us that we had no right to deny them an answer and information.

When we said we were picked up at the university, there was a murmur. "Eh, from university? It must be a serious case," said one fellow prisoner.

'My God, did you answer questions?" asked another.

When that topic seemed exhausted, a fat woman lying on a mat asked calmly, "Did you send a message to anyone to say you are here?"

"No, we did not know we would spend this long…a night… here," said Hope, breaking into tears again.

"So, how do you think you will get out of here?" the stout woman jeered.

"But…who should we have told when we don't even know what this place is called?" Hope cried. Some women laughed loudly, others smiled and a few walked away as if we were too stupid to deserve their attention.

"When a policeman comes in, ask if he can take a message for you tomorrow," the elderly lady advised. "You will need food and clothes if you are to spend more days here."

"But…surely tomorrow we will be asked about the issues that concern them, and then we will be allowed to go home," I said.

"You cannot be sure, it does no harm alerting your people," the woman replied.

Then there was noise at the door. Everyone kept quiet and looked towards the door as it was opened.

"What is the noise about?" shouted a policeman who looked at us through the bars.

Hope and I scrambled to our feet and walked shyly towards him. We explained our predicament, and he told us to write down the name of a person we wanted to be informed that we were here. "Give me the note and money tomorrow before I get off duty," he whispered, and then closed the door and quickly walked away.

We walked back to our smelly corner, and sat down.

Soon, the women began singing "Rock of ages cleft for me." Hope and I joined in. I wondered if only God could save us now.

Later, one of the prisoners pulled out an exercise book hidden behind a ventilator. It had a pen and an envelope. I paid her twenty shillings, quickly composed a letter to a friend asking for help, addressed the envelope and got out 50 more shillings to pay the policeman the next morning. Soon, our fellow prisoners began preparing for the night, pulling pieces of cloth, blankets, pillows or anything else they could find from behind ventilators and doors or other hidden places. Someone gave us a bedcover to pull over ourselves as we lay on the hard floor. Then everyone seemed to go to sleep. It was all quiet. Hope and I stayed awake for a long time, though, our minds racing with questions about how our lives had taken such an abrupt and frightening turn.

Eventually, I did nod off, but was awakened by a stir in the cell. The women were hastily hiding their improvised bedding in anticipation that the policeman soon would enter for his morning inspection. Then there was noise as the outer door of the cell opened. In came a policeman with a book. He did not say a word, but quietly looked around, counting the inmates. I handed him the envelope and money, and Hope whispered a thank you. Of course, we had no assurance he would deliver it. Entrusting him with a message was a gamble prisoners had to take.

After he left, we waited for a miracle. Surely if our friend got our note, he would get the police to release us since this was all a big mistake. Or maybe the men who picked us up would come, take us for the interview, and then let us go.

But morning turned to midday, and no angels appeared at the door.

Finally, a policeman called out for the women brought in the night before. No one had asked for our names, so no one knew who we were. Since we were the last people to be brought into the cell, we got up quickly, collected our shoes and followed the policeman, not even saying a word to the women in the cell who had kept us company over night.

Back in the reception area, the policeman ordered us to sit down. We waited, alternately yearning for someone to rescue us and dreading the thought of someone we knew seeing us so disheveled. Finally, a middle-aged man in civilian clothes came in, talked to the policeman on duty, and then ordered us to follow him.

We obeyed without hesitation or comment. We did not dare ask where we were going. We were in a trance, and each of us hoped she could wake up and ask the many questions we had.

Outside, another man joined us, leading us to another Land Rover. They ordered us to get in. With the little energy left in our bodies, we complied.

Where do you think we are going?" Hope asked me.

"I don't know. We have to wait and see. Do you think anyone knows where we are?" I whispered back.

We looked out of the vehicle windows to see if we could identify the places we were passing, still believing we were going to Ministry of Internal Affairs. But we soon saw we were moving out of town. We identified Namanve Forest where people were killed during the previous regime. Now we knew there would be no interview. Were we on our way to be killed?

Eventually, our vehicle turned onto a side road. The note we had hopefully written that morning to our friend was now useless. Even if she got the note and went to the Central Police Station to find us, no one would tell her where we were because no one knew our names. Finally, the car stopped at a gate in front of a quarter guard. A man in military uniform carrying a gun on his shoulder came out, talked to one of our captors, and then opened the gate. We drove in, and came to a stop in front of a group of soldiers, many of them armed. Our co-driver got out and talked briefly with the soldiers.

The two soldiers walked towards the vehicle. We could only watch and wait. We had nowhere to run even if we wanted to try to escape. The driver got out, opened the door, and ordered us to get out. We obeyed without hesitation. We had become used to following orders without question.

As soon as our feet touched the ground, the armed men who had walked towards the vehicle started slapping us repeatedly.

Nyinyi Wabibi wa Adui?...Eh? "Are you wives or women of the enemy?"

The slaps were so strong that we fell down crying. "Please do not beat us...What have we done?" But our questions were in vain. The men continued to kick and slap us. We could only beg for mercy or lie in the dust and hope to avoid more blows.

Then someone ordered us to move forward. We were too frightened to move fast, so the soldiers pushed, slapped and kicked us without mercy. We would fall, get up on our knees, attempt to run and fall again, absorbing kicks and blows repeatedly. At times we bumped into each other and fell, only to crawl and rise again to move ahead on the rough, uphill path. We could hear people ahead laugh and jeer every time we fell. The men who were kicking were sweating, but they were enjoying themselves.

Midway up the hill, we came to a big, army-green tent. We later learned that this was the "court house." We already had been punished as *wabibi wa adui,* but now we were going to be tried for this supposed crime. Whatever had happened to the idea of being innocent until proven guilty?

Breathless, panting, and bruised on our knees, elbows and faces, we found ourselves in the middle of a crowd of men. Most were uniformed but two or three – including the man who traveled with us but never talked to us – were in civilian dress. With final kicks, we landed half sitting and half lying in the grass, inside the big green tent, facing a bench on which about five men sat. One shouted at us, but we could not speak. We could only look at him, silently seeking mercy.

"He is asking you if you are thirsty," one of the men interpreted. The crowd laughed, apparently amused the two women who could not respond to a simple question.

"Yes," I remember responding faintly. Two men in uniform got out of the crowd and walked towards us with bottles of a colorless, clear substance. They handed the bottles to each of us. We grabbed them and eagerly gulped. Instead of the cool blessing of water, something bitter burned my mouth and throat, causing my whole body to shiver. It was the local brew known as Liralira. I saw Hope lift her bottle to return it and I did the same, but the men just laughed, and some shouted *Nywa*. "Drink!" Two men came forward. Again, I felt my weak body absorb kicks, and the men held the bottles and forced us to gulp the liquid down as the crowd cheered.

When the bottles were empty, we sat panting on the ground, and one of the men in civilian dress who was to be our judge started the examination.

"Where is your leader?"

I looked at Hope, and could only ask in a whisper to whom was the man referring.

"You cannot answer? Where are the rebels?" the man shouted, standing up and moving towards us. We had no answer, even though he threatened to kick us in our faces.

"We don't know," we both sobbed.

"You are taking us for fools!" he shouted threateningly. "Take off your clothes and see whether we will not make you tell us."

We looked at each other in disbelief. Then we looked at ourselves. We realized we already were half undressed. Our blouses were torn and open. Our instinctive reaction was to close the blouses. Surely, the judge wanted us to dress properly instead of undressing.

"I tell you to take off your clothes then you button your blouses? Who do you think you are?" he roared. This time the man kicked us. We tore off the blouses as if they were on fire and put them down, raising shaking hands to hide our breasts only partially covered now by bras.

But the men were not satisfied. "Take off everything," we were told. A man then grabbed my bra and tore it off my body. We could not think about modesty, though. We were sure we were going to be killed. There was a moment of quiet as we sat on the grass looking up at our tormentors.

"Once more, where are the rebels?" The question came again.

"Please don't kill me, I don't know," Hope said putting up her hands, this time not to hide her nakedness, but to plead for mercy.

"You will tell us,' the second judge said as he summoned with his hands two armed men to move forward.

PigaYEYE! "*B*eat her!" The uniformed men had thick wires with protruding metal ends. The first one slashed at Hope's back, and her voice let out a sound I had never heard – something between a cry and a shout. The beating continued. Blood came out of her body every time the wire came down. One of the judges ordered the man to stop beating her. She just lay there, face down, biting on her hand to stop feeling the pain from the wire.

Now it was my turn. The second man in uniform stretched the wires and ordered me to lie down straight. He beat me until the judge ordered him to stop. I was crying like a three year old. My buttocks were sore, and my thigh was bleeding where the ends of the wire had torn into flesh.

"I don't know about rebels," I cried. "Even if you kill me, there is nothing I can say." I was now lying on my side to look at my tormentor.

Moto! "Fire!" The judge gave an order to his men. I thought I was to be shot. I shouted for mercy. I looked at Hope, who was covered in blood and still lying face down. If the men could do that to her, nothing would stop them from shooting me, I thought. For some reason, I wondered on which side a bullet would hit me.

But instead of shooting, two uniformed men came and held my legs and arms, pushing me on the ground. I struggled to free myself. I wondered whether they were holding me in place in order to fire, or whether they were going to hang me. Then I saw some-one with a lighted piece of rubber coming towards me. I felt the hot rubber on my stomach, and screamed as loudly as I could. I shrieked each time a drop of rubber burnt my stomach and thighs. I tried to kick, but the men held me more firmly on the ground. I closed my eyes to avoid looking at the dropping rubber, but also to be calm and prepare to die.

When the tormentors realized I was not moving, they stopped but kept looking at me.

The two judges moved towards Hope, who was breathing unevenly. This did not stop them from kicking her.

"Get up and dress," one shouted at her when she opened her eyes. She tried to sit up and get her skirt, but she was very weak and fell down on her face.

The judge ordered uniformed men to dress her. They moved to me. A judge shouted to the men to dress me too. And then the judges walked off as if their duty was done.

The uniformed men dressed us in what was left of our attire. The shoes and little bags we had traveled with when we were taken from the university must have been taken by the armed men who were waiting for us when we arrived.

The crowd moved away as if the show was over. There was no more laughter, no more crying, no more questions and, no more pleas for mercy, at least for that day. The sun was setting and the days' work was done.

Hope and I were half dragged, half carried towards a building nearby. Inside were men and women sitting on the floor facing each other. They created room for us. Some men tried to prop us up in sitting positions so we could share the evening meal that had just been served.

"Eat, there will be no food until tomorrow this time," an inmate said.

"Please, try to eat something," another begged quietly but emphatically.

How surprising that in such harsh conditions with a bare minimum of supplies, people were eager to share. Hope swallowed one mouthful of *posho* – maize flour bread – and begged to be left alone to lie down. I managed to swallow more than two mouthfuls and to drink some bean soup thanks to an inmate who helped – actually, forced – me to swallow.

"You will die if you do not eat," the Good Samaritan whispered as he fed us both.

Hope and I were warned to make as little noise as possible, but we were too weak to talk anyway. The sunlight was fading and night was coming, although that did not make any difference to us now. Our plans to go to the market for food and to go to work the next day had vanished. We were not even thinking whether anyone knew where we were. We were in a trance because of the alcohol we were forced to drink, the torture we had undergone and the hunger and sleeplessness of the night before. Time seemed to have stopped.

At considerable discomfort to themselves, the inmates made room for us to lie down. The cell was tense with fear and pity. There were continued whispers of how badly we had been hurt. One inmate asked where we had come from. I whispered back that we were from the university. Then everyone fell silent for what could have been hours.

In the middle of the night, Hope became restless, turning from side to side and breathing heavily amidst groans. I felt sudden dread. "Is she dying?" I gasped. "She *is* dying!" But I could not see what was happening because the cell was dark.

'Shh . . ." Please keep quiet," a voice whispered in the darkness.

The groaning continued for about thirty minutes. I lay quietly and listened to my friend struggling for breath. People take it for granted when we breathe in and out without thinking about it. But it is different when one struggles for air. The groaning suddenly stopped and I screamed as audibly as I could.

"Hope . . . Hope . . . don't die."

"Please keep quiet, we have to wait till morning or we will all be killed too," a neighbor whispered.

There was silence, silence of the night. It was as if all the inmates had stopped breathing too.

I could not cry, could not talk, could not even sit up to look at my friend for a last time. I could not even exercise the God-given freedom of grieving for a friend. I had to keep quiet. I felt dead too. So I lay lifeless until what could have been morning when the door to the cell opened and let in some light.

The uniformed man looked around the room. Then someone whispered, "She is dead."

"Eh?" the guard asked, with little surprise. He moved quickly, closed the door and walked away.

There was movement in the cell as inmates sat upright, leaning against the walls to leave room for Hope who was lying on her side but with her face facing up. The light was very dim in the cell, but bright enough for all to see her lifeless position.

After a few minutes, there was noise outside the cell, and the uniformed man opened the door again, and stepped aside for two other men in uniform who entered carrying a *tundubari*, or tarpaulin. They lifted Hope's stiff body, put it on the tarpaulin, and wrapped it up. They lifted the body without a word, and carried it out, hardly glancing at the inmates. In a few minutes, the silence was broken by a car moving outside.

"They are taking her," someone whispered.

"Where?" I asked.

"Up the hill. Shh," someone whispered.

Now, my fear of dying gave way to other painful thoughts. How could I live without my friend? Would I be allowed to go for her burial? I was afraid to cry. I was afraid to offend the inmates who kept imploring me to keep quiet. There was silence again, uninterrupted silence for a long time. What sort of prison were we in where one could not even cry?

In dying, Hope may have saved my life. The next day, as I lay numb with pain and struggling to grasp my friend's fate, an official came into barracks. I already knew from my cellmates that our treatment had not been unusual, but I believe he may have been told what happened. I also learned later that human-rights advocates had noted our absence, citing us as two of a growing list of unexplained disappearances that, along with fear and mistrust arising from the guerrilla war, were coming to be part of our society's new reality. Maybe the official felt some need to exercise damage control. Whatever the reason, I soon was allowed to walk through the door into the sun.

As the fresh air helped revive my brain, a guard approached and ordered me to follow. His gun stood for death, but he also carried a powerful symbol of life – a metal water basin. I chose hope over fear, and followed. Of course, I had no choice. That had been taken from me the moment I heard the knock on the door two days earlier.

Around a corner, he put the basin down and I understood I could use it. My body gave out a sigh as I knelt down, taking first a sip, then starting to wash my filthy face. I took another sip and rested a bit, removed the remnants of my skirt and blouse, and poured the cold water over me. As I scrubbed the mud and blood from my body, hair, neck, back, stomach and legs, I realized my body was a mass of bruises and open wounds. I shivered not only from the cold, but from pain and fear. I put my clothes back on, sat leaning against a wall, folded my arms on my chest to keep warm and dozed off.

Soon, a man in civilian clothes came toward me with a syringe. Normally, I would have screamed because I fear injections, but this time I lifted my skirt to expose my bare buttocks for him. After the injection, he moved away and the guard ordered me to follow him. Obeying orders without question is not a problem when your mind is not working. I had spent two frightful days unable to get answers to any of my questions and being ignored whenever I tried to express myself. I was living in a world of zombies.

I found myself in a semi-dark room with four or five people. A man sat in the corner on the bare cement floor, his chin resting on his folded knees. He was wrapped in a bed sheet. A body lay at one side, curled up like a puppy underneath a threadbare blanket. It was emaciated, and I could not tell whether it was male or female, young or old. In the barracks there were no men or women, no young or old. All were God's creatures. This one had sunken cheeks and big white eyes that seemed about to fall out of their sockets. It emitted an unbearable stench. I looked away to hide my fear, and saw a woman lying along another wall wrapped in a *gomesi*. She looked at me without bothering to move or utter a word. I saw another body lying on the floor facing the wall; it was covered with a big trench coat.

"You are shivering," a voice under the big coat said. The figure rose and covered me with the coat. In the warmth, I nodded off to sleep.

Slowly, life in my new cell assumed an odd normalcy. I got an injection every day, and my wounds started to heal. The guards were not hostile, and allowed us to go out into the sunshine. The inmates shared the few resources they had. I could borrow a *lesu* from one to wrap around my body so that I could wash my one skirt. But I always had to put it on before it dried.

The odor from the ghost-like man came from many septic wounds and urine he passed uncontrollably. He was always complaining and finding fault with every one – especially those who refused to take his smelly bedding into the sun to air out. Despite his ghastly appearance, he was the epitome of vanity. "It is sad that I am sharing a space with people like you," he would sneer at his cellmates. He was illiterate but rich, and had thrived during the military dictatorship. But then he was beaten up by unnamed enemies, and thrown into the barracks. Money is important, but not in prison and in death. Those two equalizers treat us all alike.

I helped him a lot. In exchange, he warned me not to confide too much in the lady who had given me the coat on my first day in this cell. He said she was a spy. The other inmates had heard that Hope and I had collaborated with the guerrilla movement that was threatening to take over the government. I had nothing to hide, but I found myself afraid to talk with the lady even though she had shown me kindness in one of my lowest moments. She was the real *adui*, or enemy, I decided.

The woman in *gomesi* was popular in the cell because she had a Christian book of the apostle Jude Tadeo – a book with prayers. The inmates believed that wishes and prayers are fulfilled for those who say a particular one of these prayers seven times a day for seven days.

As weeks turned into months, I decided to try it out although it was not in my religious teachings. I put my fate into God's hands. All the inmates had given their lives to God – but not through songs, prayer, confession or testimonies. Inmates were afraid to talk about God because the guards were always listening and we feared reprisal. There are issues men tell God but do not want people who are not close to know. So we all quietly prayed that God could get us out alive.

During the three months I spent in the cell, only one inmate was released. When guards called him out of the cell, we thought he was getting visitors or maybe would be given food sent by relatives. But the guards told him he would be set free. He asked to return to the cell to pick up his shoes. When he returned, the other inmates laughed at him. *Ori musiru..bwebakuzamu!* "Are you a fool, what if they put you inside again?" one shouted. He quickly left, and I lost an opportunity to give him a message to carry to the outside world.

Christmas came. Some cows were brought into the compound and shot so they could be slaughtered for distribution to the military men. The inmates were lucky to share a meal of meat and *posho* on that special day. But inmates had given up hope of living normal lives again. Guards told stories of many people who had been killed, their bodies taken into a forest on top of the hill. Our hearts raced whenever a vehicle came into the barracks at night, and we dreaded being called out lest that meant we were marked to die.

One night, there were many gunshots from within the barracks. We could not tell where they were coming from, but we kept quiet because we feared our cell would be targeted next. The next day, some inmates were taken to the quarter-guard to clean up. There were no people and no bodies – just blood.

I borrowed the book from the woman in *gomesi,* and studied it diligently. I realized that having a relationship with God would give me confidence and hope for protection. God knew the rich and the poor, the educated and the illiterate, those who were armed and those who suffered at the hands of the armed and could not defend themselves. Like all prisoners, I believed God would answer my prayers in His time. In the meantime, after three months surrounded by guards with guns, living on one evening meal a day, never having soap or bed sheets, and wearing the same, single set of tattered clothes, I had learned that life is not about luxuries. It is about being able to breathe free, God-given air without difficulty.

One afternoon, after I had been reading the Jude Tadeo for just under seven days, a Land Rover entered the barracks. I was called out, escorted to it and ordered to get in without explanation. I was not excited. I only felt fear wondering where I would be taken next.

My destination turned out to be Luzira maximum-security prison. We drove through the gate, stopped, and I was led from the vehicle to reception, where a warder was waiting.

"Take her in on detention," my guard said.

"Where did you get her from?" the female warder, asked as she got out a book and started to write.

"From Central Police Station," the man replied without hesitation.

From the floor where I had been ordered to sit, I nearly screamed to deny this falsehood, but I controlled myself and kept quiet. I had learned to keep quiet and not to believe everything I heard. The gentleman said goodbye to the warder and went away without looking back at me. The warder pulled a chair next to where I was seated and asked me more questions – about my name, age, what I used to do before the arrest.

For most people, entering a maximum security prison would be frightful. But I was overjoyed. It was as if I was joining a secondary school again. I had never been a real prisoner. Like all the other inmates at the barracks, I had been put through no procedures to make me one. No charges had been brought against me. There was no register to show who I was and why I was there. I had been solely there at God's mercy. Now I had a name and an official record. With my name written in a big black book, no one would make me disappear. At least someone someday would tell my parents, friends and siblings where I was.

I felt nothing but joy as I was led to a dormitory with double-decker beds and given a uniform. God had answered my prayers.

In prison, I found myself among women who had many different stories. Some had worked in the regime of the previous dictator and were being held to help the government get to the wrongdoers. Some had been arrested for embezzlement or for being accomplices to people who stole money, mainly from banks. Then there were others like me who did not know what their crime was.

My relatives learned I was in prison and came to visit me. They brought me food, soap and creams, as if they were visiting a schoolgirl. They hired a lawyer, who heard my story. He could only say my detention had been illegal. But he failed to get me a court appearance. There was no one accusing me of anything, so I could not be tried. It was the state that had detained me.

I spent another three months in this new prison. Then, just as mysteriously as that knock on the door that began the whole nightmare, I was called into the prison warders' office and told I was free to go home. I was given a document and money for bus fare. And so I walked back into the outside world that I had forgotten and that had forgotten me. I left as I had arrived – never charged, never tried, never allowed to face my accusers and be adjudicated.

I now had two alternatives – to stay in Uganda or to flee into exile as many people were doing. I chose to stay. I picked up the pieces of my life and moved on. But I carried with me a searing awareness of the suffering just beyond my everyday life – of countless women who are raped and forgotten in war and defiled and shunned in peace, and of millions more who are brutalized by poverty and trafficked for sex, surrogacy or body parts in supposedly good times.

To me, these are no longer theoretical injustices done to unseen people. They are tangible realities that can happen anytime, anywhere and to anyone. And concepts like rule of law are no longer fancy abstractions found in textbooks. They are absolute moral imperatives.

No Time for Pain

By Harriet Anena

You are lying on the couch in your living room, listening to Relentless by Hillsong United. You've been playing it since 8 am when you dragged yourself out of bed. It's now 2 pm and you're still cooped up, your eyes roving from the TV to the laptop and back to a book you've been reading for two weeks now.

You should be having lunch, but the thought of eating alone keeps hunger at bay. Eating is one thing that fails to fit in your solitary life.

It has been four years since you graduated from Makerere University, left Gulu and relocated to Kampala where a job awaited you. You have an even better job now, pay your bills, have a plot of land to your name, live in a house your friends admire, and your family knows they can count on you. Your bank account is decent, and you can always provide a little help to friends in need.

Still, you can't understand why simply putting food in your mouth gives you trouble. You can't understand why hunger eludes you even though an emptiness continues to reside in your stomach – an emptiness that isn't a result of hunger but rather a result of something ignored.

You remember the day you went to see the doctor, your body sucked dry of energy and your head spinning. You expected a clear diagnosis, but the doc said nothing was wrong. "You just need to get someone to live with – a sister or a friend," he had said. "Stay around people."

You were happy the doctor didn't say you were sick. But you weren't happy with his recommended "treatment." Loud people and crowds freak you out. You love loneliness.

Grudgingly, you had started dancing in front of the mirror. You worked out. And you wrote. You wrote down anything that came to your mind – anything you saw, anything you felt, anything you heard, even if it was just an echo…

At 4 pm you remember that an ulcer gave you a beating the previous month. Keeping that tummy empty will surely invite it back. So you go to the kitchen, serve yourself a plate of *lapena* and *layata* and eat – slowly. When you're done eating, you put the book down, open a new page on the laptop and type.

> *Loneliness is my loyal companion*
> *It never breaks our bond. It never leaves…*

Outside, your neighbors' children are playing football. They scream and laugh, shove and pull each other. Then they quarrel in a language made in South Sudan. You don't understand a word, but you want to be them. Better yet, you want to travel to 1997 when Gulu Public was your primary school. You want to be 10 years old again. You want your best friend to still be Cathy Acen, your partner in mischief.

The two of you were on your way home from school, but the sky was grumbling. Thick dark clouds hung low, threatening to release torrents of rain any minute. You stood under the Olam Tree in Cereleno watching people dash in all directions, afraid the impending rain would trap them on the streets.

You placed your books in black polythene bags, and strapped them on your backs. You thought the books would be safe from the rain that way. Then fat droplets began to pelt you with vigor as they fled their cage in the sky.

As the rain continued to pour, you started a slow walk home. There were no vehicles in sight, so you stood in the middle of the road and looked up toward the sky. You let the rain scour your faces.

You ran, walked, ran and walked until you reached Layibi Centre. You stood there, listening to the water gushing through a culvert and flowing onto a nearby garden. You dashed to the exit of the culvert, and you giggled as running water slapped your legs.

You let your voices tear through the thunder and moans of the sky as you celebrated the rain. When you reached the railway crossing, you stopped playing because Acen had arrived at her home and because most people in the area knew you. You didn't want them to see you playing in the rain.

You said your goodbyes and continued the one-kilometer journey home alone.

You wake with a start. Your attention is drawn to the hummingbird pecking at its reflection on your window. It's been doing this for the past three days, every 6:30 am. You like birds. But you don't understand this daily visit.

Then you look around and realize you'd slept off on the couch. For how long, you don't want to know. You love sleep. The TV is blinking; you left it on. The book you had been reading sits dejected next to the table, and your laptop is in hibernation.

It's Monday – never an easy day of the week. But you're happy because you'll be at work again. You'll be around people – people who make you dress up in another attire of life. With work, you can forget about the loneliness and silence in your house – a silence that sometimes becomes so loud you sing back at it in that voice that made you lead singer at Sacred Heart Secondary School. Work makes you shelve your fear of darkness. Work makes you focus on the here and now.

You walk to the bedroom, sit on the edge of the bed and stare at the suitcase of clothes. You wonder what you'll wear today. Short clothes do it for you these days. They make you feel sexy and rebellious. So you iron the short strapless dress and a jacket to go with it.

When you're done, you sip hot water mixed with cinnamon, honey and vinegar – your addiction. Then you eat two sweet bananas. You love them. You take a glass of water and head out. The hummingbird leaves too.

Ten minutes later, you're in office, and your day is defined by research, putting together an article, calls, emails, planning and more.

Then it's 5 pm. You know you should go home, but you stay put. Your mind starts travelling. Words trail it at every turn. You jot them down, and give birth to a new life, a new poem. You like these moments when words rescue you.

Forty-five minutes later, you make up your mind to go home, in time for your evening jog. Jogging unclogs your mind. You sleep better, wake up feeling sharp. For today's run, you'll brave that hill you've been dodging. With your running shoes on, you start with short brisk steps, cross the road and begin the slow, determined run up the hill.

This is a quiet neighborhood – Bunga. You pass by lines of apartments and mansions that all look dead. A car appears from behind thick walls and screeches past you; the driver's eyes linger on you from the rear mirror. A dog barks faintly at the tap-tap of your footsteps; city dogs don't know what real barking is. Children look down from the balcony, and scream, "Yay! Yay! Yay!" You run past some men; they look at you from head to toe, and turn to look at your backside. You know because one is asking the other why you're jogging when your body doesn't need it; the words land on your back. But you're happy – happy for the sweat stroking your skin, happy that you have conquered the hill, happy because your body and you are on the same page.

Back home, you sit on the floor. The cold tiles are a contrast to the heat pounding under your skin. You let your mind leave your body and travel to good times, like that day in 2003.

You were seated under the mango tree shade on a Saturday afternoon, the radio bellowing Leeo Pa Layeng's Amaro Nyinga – "I love my name." Then Akello started reading announcements on Mega FM. You didn't pay much heed until she said "writing competition." You realized too late you'd missed out on details. You waited for the 9 pm announcement, and listened again; Acholi Religious Leaders Peace Initiative had organized a writing competition ahead of the Day of the African Child. Essays or poems were expected. You were excited.

That night, you lay on your back, stared at the roof and let your mind wander for hours. Early morning the next day, you sat on the verandah, as your mind pushed forth a newborn poem.

When the results came out, you were a winner. The victory came with a bursary, so you didn't have to worry about lack of fees for A-level. You were thrilled. At Gulu Central High School, you worked hard as though your fees were being paid by the clan. You whipped brains in class. You soared.

Thinking about all that now, you find yourself smiling as the lines of that winning poem fall in place in your mind.

The sun rises and sheds its rays upon the earth
The wind blows through hills and valleys
Bringing hope for us all –
But not so for the Acholi child.

Born in the bush,
Living in protected camps
Year in, year out—twenty and over
Surrounded by terrors in a land of misfortune,
Weeping and mourning are life companions.

AIDS robbed us of parental love and care
We face brutality, abduction
And are sexually molested by our protectors.

Landless, parentless,
Denied health and quality education,
Yet still we scratch our destiny
From the hands of a curtailing fate.

The poem snaps you out of your reverie, forcing to the front of your mind a history you want to erase. It stares you in the face. You head to the shower, seek the soothing warmth to wash away cold memories of that day in 1994.

You were at Grandma's home. Susan, Irene, Carol and Emily had come home from Entebbe for December holidays. A bunch of other children from Gulu were around. Grandma's home was brimming with children and adults, with activity and words and little joys that only village life can offer.

At night, you huddled with five or six children on several papyrus mats, everyone sharing a blanket. You never really knew what took place in the night; you didn't listen to any sounds because when you slept, you slept properly.

You slept with the exhaustion of children who had spent the day hunting birds, running to the swamp to pick sugarcane, joining the adults in the garden to harvest groundnuts or maize, or sitting around the fireplace listening to Grandma tell Ododo about the hare and the tortoise: "Let's see whose mother can float on water," the hare had said. "The tortoise, showing that he's up to the challenge, wrapped his mother neatly and threw her in the water. She drowned. The hare on the other hand, threw a mortar in the water instead and it floated away. When the tortoise discovered the hare's mischief, he planned a deadly revenge that the hare would forever remember...

Later that night, when silence had settled upon Layibi, something happened.

Guns were fired.

"Wake up now! Fast!" Grandma whispered urgently.

She was bending over you, shaking you. Your legs started trembling. Your palms were instantly damp. You squatted behind the door, trembling like chicks picked out of a pool of water.

What's going on? Where are we going?

"Lukwena," Grandma had said, as though she'd read your minds.

You headed for the bushes as gunfire between Joseph Kony's rebels and the Ugandan army soldiers violated the night. You ran, stumbled, fell, got up and ran again. You maneuvered through potato gardens, swamps and fields. You didn't feel thorn pricks, the hurt from a fall or the thrust of a toe against stone. There was no time for pain. It was only later, when you took shelter under the Odugu Tree, that you became aware of the pain bedeviling your skins. You crowded together to keep away the cold, and waved in the air to chase away mosquitoes. You had invaded their territory.

"We'll be safe here," Grandma had said.

You believed her.

But things were not the same again. You slept every night in the Alup - a makeshift shelter Daddy erected at the swamp. The Alup, big enough for Daddy, Mama and your four siblings, became your home after dark. In the Alup, mosquitoes gave you a beating, and frogs croaked endlessly.

You imagined a snake sneaking in between the dry banana leaves that formed the wall of your shelter. And you imagined rebels abducting or killing you all on one of their night raids. You imagined all that and more. You held onto your blankets, shut your eyes tightly even when sleep stayed away, and you prayed for the sun to rise and find you still breathing. When sun rays slipped through the slits of banana leaves of your Alup the next morning, you breathed aloud, pinched yourself a bit to be sure you were alive. You smiled, even if the smile was limping.

Yet you were grateful. Living in the Alup was better than relocating to the camps where the rest of your people would later be herded. In the Alup, you didn't have to queue up for yellow beans and posho, for cooking oil and salt, for saucepans and jerry cans from Red Cross and UN people. And each morning when you awoke safe, you sighed with relief because you knew there was still school. Even if you studied for only five or six hours a day instead of eight, you knew it was better than camp life, where school was a garden where rebels harvested children to become gunmen.

You were happy because your family didn't have to carry a pot of shame as they begged for food and shelter from strangers. You were happy your home was not far from town. If it were deep in the village, camp life would be the only option. Lukwena loved villages – the raids, abductions and killings were easier there, away from the timid glare of government soldiers.

You got used to the Alup. You looked forward to it. You didn't mind trekking the long distance from home to the swamp every day for a decade, with a papyrus mat and a blanket under your arm. You didn't complain, even though mosquitoes gave you malaria every so often. You understood when Lapit's wife stuffed a piece of cloth in her baby's mouth so the sound of its sobbing wouldn't travel far and attract the rebels. You also knew that the sun brought hope every morning. Hope meant you were alive and well. But the sun brought hopelessness too, because daylight confirmed that some people didn't rise with the sun like you.

For a long time, you didn't ask why elders spoke in hushed tones, why names were not uttered aloud, and why children were not expected to scream or play. But at some point, you started asking questions, asking God why your life and that of the people in this part of the country were different. You even asked him what he did every evening when you headed to the Alup. Your questions got even more pointed when you and your family sat around the radio and heard news about the mayhem of Kony and his men.

You became fed up. So you and your family decided you'd sleep at home one night. The next morning, the compound was littered with footprints of Lukwena. The rebels had abducted children in the area, but for some unknown reason walked past your home. From that day on, you never asked any questions. You resumed sleeping in the Alup until 2006 when the two lions –Kony and the president he was fighting to replace – decided it was time for guns to go to sleep; these beasts had waged a war for power since 1987, using children, women, young men and even the unborn as shields. For twenty years, they decreed that the best place for a people were the "internally displaced persons" camps. They smashed the eggs of peace against rocks, and watched as many of their own people breathed their last. Then as abruptly as they had started the war, they decided they needed a break.

How you celebrated! Even if no peace pact was signed, you were happy that the fear that ripped your heart as you tiptoed to school every day via the railway line would be gone. You rejoiced that camps would be no more, and that children would be spared their daily commute from villages to Gulu Bus Park or Kaunda Grounds for safety.

You are a proud people, the Acholi. You live off your sweat. But this war had taken that away and with the guns silent, you were excited about searching for your lost dignity that lay beneath the rubble of war.

You stand a little longer under the shower, then step out, towel yourself and go to bed. You'll miss dinner today – you don't feel like it. Your mind is exhausted from wandering. You like it that way because sleep won't take long to come. When it does, you allow it to take charge.

The phone vibrates against your arm and you are awake. You avoid your phone these days. It has been a month since you released your poetry collection – A Nation in Labour – and the feedback is overwhelming.

Comments of "Well done," "Go girl," and "Proud of you" adorn your Facebook wall. Friend requests and messages stream in past midnight, and you just can't comprehend how to deal with it all. You're happy but you're not used to this kind of attention and praise. You're uncomfortable too, because some people, after reading your name and seeing your mugshot on the book cover, say, "You don't look like them." And when you explain, they say, "You don't speak like them." "Them" refers to your people – the Acholi people – who are supposed to have an accent of their own, are supposed to be tall, dark, look militant and have short kinky hair. In the face of such comments, you have to make justifications about who you are and why you are the way you are.

Once they're convinced you really are one of them, more questions come. How did you survive the war? Did you actually live in an IDP camp? Did you see the rebels? How about Kony? What do you think about this ICC thing and Dominic Ongwen? You try your best to remain calm and offer explanations about your life, the International Criminal Court and the abducted child who would become a rebel commander. Such discussions always end with a sigh. Then comes odd praise for having climbed the ladder of a curtailing life to become someone. That leaves you speechless.

You push aside those thoughts and suddenly droplets of happiness tap-tap at your skin because last evening you decided to travel home. You'll be in Layibi where you don't need to explain yourself, your name, your history, your present. It has been two months since you last went home.

By 1 pm, you're aboard Homeland Bus. After six hours on the road, you are in Gulu. You take a boda boda from Layibi Centre to Cubu where home has always been. When you arrive, Mama is seated under the mango tree, peeling cassava.

Mama's words, like yours, are few, but even in those counted words, you feel her countless joy at seeing you.

You sit next to her on the papyrus mat. She's not the Mama who used to whip you for coming late from school and for putting too much salt in the sauce. Now you talk about all sorts of things – work, home, life in the city, men and even how she used to beat you.

You laugh. You eat the *gwana* from Kafu and *labolo* from Luweero that you always take home. You talk. She gives you all the updates about the weddings, deaths, child births, elopements, pregnancies, defilements, thefts that happened while you were away.

Then you get an update about what the village wind feels like on your skin – the wind that's not polluted, the wind that's not too rough. You get an update about what real food tastes like –food that's not too spicy, not too junky. You get an update on what family is like – a family that's not too broken, not too scattered. And you feel the kind of contentment that comes from the base of your stomach, not the type that resides on the tip of the tongue.

In the evening, the whole family is around, even those married and living distances away and those taken away by education or work. It's one family – a family seated on a disturbing past, but holding the hands of promising tomorrows.

The next day, you head to Gulu town, to catch up with old friends. As you stop by Centenary Bank, a woman seated by the roadside just in front of the bank catches your attention. She is in her late forties and she's is a beggar.

Konya do latina. "Help me, my child."

You wonder how long she has sung that song. You wonder what happened to her home, to her family. You wonder what made her this vulnerable. When you're done withdrawing money, you walk past her, your eyes fixed straight ahead, your ears closed to her pleas. You don't believe in giving to beggars, especially the able-bodied ones.

At Carla Store, where you have gone to buy a notebook, you meet a blind, elderly woman being led by a small boy about eight years old. They stand at the counter, their focus on the store keeper and their voices rising above the traffic from the street nearby.

Konya do latina, konya do, the woman pleads.

You turn away, buy the notebook and start heading out. Then you stop at the doorway, turn back and ask the boy which school he goes to. He dropped out in Primary Four. You don't ask him more questions; you're not ready to listen to a sad tale this morning. You give him some money and go your way, leaving them there, the sightless eyes of a grandmother and the sharp eyes of grandson staring at the shopkeeper. He'll probably give them a bar of soap or sugar or salt. That's what they usually give on Fridays, the day for "needy" elders – a practice that's the offspring of war.

The two women remind you of Grandma. But unlike them, Grandma, despite her arthritis, still insists on collecting grass for the cows, adding firewood to the stove, peeling potatoes. They remind you of Mama, who still tends to her garden and goes to her town job religiously.

When the day comes for you to head back to the city, you're rejuvenated and joyful. But you're also sad that the seed of *konya do latina* that was planted during the 20 years of camp life continues to grow in the hearts of people who got used to free yellow posho and weevil-ridden beans.

Your heart becomes a cracked shell as you look outside the bus window and see a 10-year-old girl vending *labolo* on a school day and another with his hand held out to you, his teenage voice singing *konya do*.

But you also feel happy as you pass Cereleno – that place where water slapped your feet. You see a bakery, and across the road are carpenters making chairs, tables, beds, coffins.

You are happy that in Layibi Centre, salons line the street, women in Layibi Market laugh aloud in celebration of the day's sales, grinding mills roar nearby and farmers from Koro, Palenga and Opit bring sacks of beans, passion fruit, charcoal, okra and chicken for sale.

You watch dust rise as Homeland Bus gathers speed, and you know that when that dust settles, the seed of resilience will be more visible – that people like you will continue to run faster than the shadow of yesterday, and skeletons of the past will keep fading.

It's Complicated

By Lydia Namubiru

I was in the final stages of applying for a job with an American non-profit organization. The interviews, though arduous, had gone well, and we were down to negotiating salary and checking references. I was getting excited about moving to a bigger city and, most importantly, about taking on challenging work that fit my skills and aspirations like a glove. But then things went badly awry.

First, I took umbrage at a demand that I provide my prospective employer access to my bank records – an intrusion for which nobody could give a sensible explanation. My objections earned me a 30-minute verbal assault from the organization's country representative, a fellow African. He reproached my behavior as "a very African thing." But what really brought the application to a screeching halt was a call from one of my references, an American who had supervised me in an earlier job. My prospective employers had asked her a question I doubt they could have asked an African: "Did I hate *muzungu* bosses?" It seems they had gleaned as much from my blog, a running monologue in which I whine about virtually every aspect of my life. I went back and read through all 67 posts, and I could find just two lines expressing any opinion on *muzungus* at all – a joke that my *muzungu* bosses were working me as if I too were an expatriate without a life outside my work, and a comment that we Africans were "tired (*twakoowa*) of *muzungu* interventionism."

In that clannish way that westerners in the Africa-aid sector tend to treat each other, my former boss sympathized with those who now held my fate in their hands. "Why do you want this kind of work?" she demanded. "Just for career advancement? Do you believe in the people who are doing it? "If not, why don't you go start something of your own – something African?"

That did it. Even though I stood to double my salary, the new job wasn't worth it. So I withdrew my application. How dare they presume to set up shop in my neighborhood, and then tell me that if I didn't like it, I should go open my own shop further down the street?

I never told my former or prospective employer why I turned down the job or what I really thought about *muzungus*. But if I had, I might have explained that my feelings towards westerners, the western world and its involvement in Africa are a rather complicated landscape.

I have known many westerners. I love some, am indifferent to some and despise others – the same range of opinions I hold for fellow Africans. I grew up on American television soap operas – an enviable world where people are rich and without real problems. They spend their days chasing love and sex. By default they have successful companies, white mansions, sleek cars and pretty faces. I have never been to the west, so I am going to stick with that impression until proven otherwise.

When I came to know westerners personally, I found myself transported to a place of civil and individual liberties and political systems that manage to elevate more Barack Obamas, Bill Clintons, Angela Merkels and Tony Blairs than despots and thieves. Where streets are wide and clean. Where economies are so productive that people can afford to meet not only their basic needs but have enough left over to create magnificent, life-enriching things like Broadway. Where an unwavering spirit of innovation has produced everything from the Industrial Revolution to Silicon Valley's modern miracles. A place where opportunities seem to sprout right from the streets, and a person's most cherished dreams can come true as long as she gives it a try.

Also, the western world gave me my best childhood friends – Oliver Twist, Tom Sawyer, Huckleberry Finn, the Hardy Boys, the Famous Five, and one person even more beloved than these. I met him when I was about eight years old, and was just graduating from tales about Mr. Fox and Mr. Frog. It was a school holiday, and I was spending the three weeks at my grandmother's house in the village so that my parents could get a break from city expenses. On the shelf, someone more literate than my grandmother had left a dusty little book without a cover or the preface pages. On the first page of what was left I read, "My name is David Copperfield."

Thus I tumbled into 17th century England, a world where adults were "firm" with children – in other words, cruel, much as in 20th century Uganda. I cried so hard and so long at the misery in those pages that my grandmother cut short my village stay, and sent me back to my mother. Imagine my confusion when my mother told me David wasn't real. To illustrate the phenomenon of novels further, she brought Oliver Twist into my life. I identified so strongly with this lad and my other newfound literary friends that in my mind Oliver Twist was black, the Hardy Boys were discovering villains right around the corner of the compound where I lived, the fence Tom Sawyer had to whitewash cut right across my parents' yard and the adventures of The Famous Five were often set in my grandmother's banana plantation.

To this day, the western world still serves up my most loved artistic expression. How much poorer my life would be if I hadn't been introduced to Andrew Lloyd Weber, Oscar Hammerstein or Richard Rodgers. And I still love a good, sappy, American TV show; I have happily given many hours of my life to *Grey's Anatomy*. I do think the west's current popular music scene is a crap heap, but I have to admit that tunes by Lionel Richie, R Kelly or even 50 Cent have inexplicably thrilled me on many a night out. Yes, the western world is still the land of my fantasies.

But I would never choose to live in the west – and not just because I couldn't endure the cold months. For one thing, I could never survive the western clock. Westerners are obsessed with it. While I am not proud of the tardiness rampant in my culture, I prefer it to being enslaved to time. Of course, the culture of squeezing as much into every minute as is humanly possible helps westerners accomplish many things; I suspect it accounts for much of the West's advantage in material wealth. While westerners invest their time, Africans simply use ours. But I refuse to let supposedly "urgent" needs force me to cram more into every hour and rob me of the freedom to enjoy the quality of my everyday life – the warm feel of the sun, the soothing breeze, and especially the many unexpected encounters with people that make each day an adventure. And if I had to stop having friendly, non-work conversations with my colleagues in order to be more productive, I would not know and enjoy them as much as I do now. Inevitably, they – or even youth itself – would move on, and I would have missed something important. That's too high a price to pay for material wealth.

I also don't think I would have many girlfriends in the West. By all accounts, the West is the best place in the world to be a woman. I grew up wanting to be like a western woman – or at least the version of her I saw in the soaps. On television, at least, the western woman is pretty, strong and aggressive. She takes the world by the horns, and bows to no man. She has her own businesses, or at least holds a powerful position in the company where she works. She drives a car, wears power heels and doesn't stay home being hassled by children. She can and does do whatever she wants. When I was growing up, she struck me as everything real African mothers weren't. I long wanted to be like her, not my mother.

But now I say, "No thanks." Having known western women personally, I think they often tend to be crass, unnecessarily competitive, high strung and quite often obstructive over-organizers. I have seen them treat virtues I have long cultivated and value – like humility and quietness – as if they were vices. They say I am too meek. As if trying to fix my deformities, they take me under their wings, and attempt to teach me to be "tough." A female American boss once said to me, "You are intelligent, passionate and have a lot of potential. But you need to have more professional presence." Another time, a Canadian superior boasted that she was "loud and energetic," and told me: "I want to see some spirit in you."

Yes, I may have dreamed of being a western woman when I was growing up, but I was raised by an African mother to be an African woman. As a result, while holding the western feminist ideals in my breast, I don't wear the battle armor. I am definitely not loud; I was taught that is rude. Until I have something I am convinced needs to be said, I won't speak. It is not a lack of confidence. I just happen to have been taught that it is more helpful. I make no apologies for how I turned out.

The condescension I find in western women's attitude toward me is mirrored in a big way by how western organizations – especially governments and charitable organizations – approach my society. They are everywhere, with their monstrously big vehicles branded in screaming self-praise, "saving lives, bringing hope, defeating poverty." I have been a part of their machinery: I worked three years with international nongovernment organizations. Yet I would be hard-pressed to find evidence that poverty has been defeated even by an inch, or that lives have been saved or changed enough to justify half their investment – even though I worked in evaluation departments.

Sure, western organizations produce some touching stories: a farmer whose chickens were saved thanks to advice sent to his phone by an NGO, mothers who get the out-of-reach and potentially life-saving opportunity to deliver their babies in hospitals using vouchers paid for by an NGO, a 16-year old girl who avoids another pregnancy thanks to the contraceptive services of one NGO, and a whole population of HIV-positive people who get care from NGOs. But for the amount of money and human capacity invested, the west's current way of involvement in Africa is dumbfoundingly flawed. I felt like a fraud citing those anecdotal stories when I knew that the text message that saved the chicken cost $10, while a commercial outfit operating in a one-room office somewhere in Kampala was sending out messages for just 10-cents apiece – and earning a profit. Or that while an NGO spent $28 to give the young girl contraception, private clinics in a different, equally remote part of the country were giving the same service for just $8.

I left journalism to join the NGO sector because I thought NGOs were problem solvers, the ones that got their hands dirty finding and implementing solutions. But what I found was an overwhelmingly complicated and intricate organizational system of core funders, cost-sharing partners, implementing partners, headquarter teams, field teams, senior managers, directors, vice presidents, junior vice presidents, service teams, support teams, business development teams and on and on. I had thought the problems of my country were simple: people needed access to essential medicine, better information and the like. But I found an organizational complex that seemed to have been transplanted from another planet. A western NGO would try to extract a jigger using the super-modern, high-tech da Vinci robotic surgical system even though tweezers and a needle would do. Why? Perhaps because the west itself is a huge organizational system so their solutions always come with baggage. But self-interest also plays a big role. A large percentage of western aid is sunk into rent and salaries of western experts sent to "build our capacity" to run that robot. If the robot weren't alien and complex enough, it would be hard for western donors to justify the money that goes out of foreign citizens' taxes into the pockets of foreign clients.

And the experts come in droves. They drive rents in nice neighborhoods so high that landlords start quoting them in dollars. In our fertile land where markets are brimming with fresh fruit, they demand packaged dry fruits, so our supermarkets stock up on them. They patronize coffee shops, and for this we are grateful. They demand Internet access, and it comes to town. Thanks again. But in the meantime, something pernicious happens. We, the local staff, learn of the high western salaries, and demand more for ourselves. We get double or even triple the salaries the local capitalists around us would ever offer. So we chase NGO jobs and play interested students. We learn how to create donor-quality

PowerPoint presentations, use special phone apps to book meetings, share our calendars online and draw up elaborate Excel work plans. We gain "capacity" in being organized and structured. We get psyched about the change our organizations are making in the world. In the words of one of my self-appointed NGO mentors, we come to "own the attitude."

In reality, the money that is flowing in to prop us all up is causing inflation and creating a wealthy, but for the most part unproductive, cadre of Ugandans who feed on NGOs. I know. I was one. We go down "to the ground" to implement our employers' unexamined solutions. The people at the grassroots have lost their patience for us. They refuse to come for our "community sensitization" meetings. So like good students of western ways, we pay local people generous "transport refunds" so they will come learn about how they can change their lives. To outsiders, the strategy appears to work. The locals come to their meetings to collect their payments. Once there, the donors try to sell their latest bright ideas. Then the locals let the outsiders in to implement them.

NGOs' projects may or may not achieve much success, but they have departments to crunch numbers and creatively weave words to tout their achievements with slogans like "Eight Million Lives Touched Globally." Do you want a donor-backed project to prove that its touching had an impact? How much money do you have? For half a million dollars, they can get a Yale professor to do a randomized control trial that tells you whether or not their $5 million achieved impact. The expert's methods are very solid. They represent a new science. They can tell you exactly how much of the change can be attributed to the NGO's work. Of course, you can also go to the National Bureau of Statistics and find data that says the people in the communities we serve remain really poor, but then you can't expect a single project to defeat poverty.

Oops, I forgot the NGO's slogan! I think we just need to "build the capacity" of that bureau to collect valid data. You should talk to the country director of that local affiliate of an international NGO across town. Maybe she met someone in her yoga class who has the right skill set for the job. Oh, of course she knows someone – a very impressive young man she met at the country club. At 28, he already has a Harvard MBA. Yes, she'll talk to the director of the bureau about him. Her organization is currently funding their pilot on collecting market prices. Yes, the young man is going to be very useful to the bureau indeed. Everyone complains about the quality of data coming out of the place.

As a friend (and fellow NGO alumna) said in the weeks after I left that world, "It is bullshit – manufactured bullshit."

It can be argued that prostitution is better than marrying a man for his money, and so it can be argued that colonialism was better than the current system of benevolence with which the west is subduing Africa. Prostitutes and colonialists surely are morally repulsive, but at least they are honest about their intentions. For prostitutes, love is a simple business transaction. Colonialism was pretty straightforward too: the West wanted raw materials, so it went out and took other people's land to get them.

I don't know the full intentions for which the west keeps throwing its money at Africa today. I just know that the self interest of both westerners and Africans keeps the machinery growing in size and intricacy. So what if the charity that rains down on Africa like manna from heaven obstructs organic development stifles local innovation and creativity and negates the need for the growth of a good work ethic? So what if this props up bad governments by plugging holes in their service delivery with loose mud? So what? After all, western leaders get to make their electorate feel good about how their tax money is helping abroad, and African leaders get to mask some of their own failings.

While colonialism was immoral and wrong on a thousand and one fronts, at least Africans could be mad about it. Eventually we kicked it out, without worrying about grey areas. Also, it did spur a certain amount of growth. To transport their raw material produce, colonialists built roads and railways. To avoid social anarchy as a result of rebellion against the obvious wrongs of colonialism, they built police institutions. Eventually they even built nations – nations that continue to exist, albeit with myriad problems. Yes, colonialists were unjust and exploitative. They advanced their interests at the expense of local communities. But that was nothing new. All kinds of governments, from the pre-colonial monarchies through colonial administrations to the thieving so-called democracies of today have all exploited or disregarded the likes of me to benefit the few. I have come not to care a terrible lot about the race of the oppressor.

So there it is – my belated answer to prospective western employer who thought I might have problems with *muzungu* bosses. It is not one of those questions for which you can force a yes or no answer.

It's complicated.

Metallic Glory

By Elvania M. Bazaala

Time check: 0800hours. Oops, I overslept again.

That is my first conscious thought as Mama's loud voice bounces off the surfaces of our small house, reminding me of school regulations and the responsibilities of a young lady to respect time. I rise and put my feet on the floor, only to feel my muscles protest, painfully reminding me of the previous day's activities and begging me to grant them a few minutes to warm up for the day.

Moments like these defined my early years. Perhaps the end justifies the means, but it's the beginning that gives a soul reason to pursue an end. For me, the starting line became visible at age 8: I was drawn to train and compete as an athlete. Why I developed this burning ambition remains a mystery I cannot put into words. All I know is that woman is slave to her passions – passions that for me were spelled out by dreams that I saw whether I was awake or asleep. I had no option. I decided to start running. I ran to catch up with other children and to beat the clock so I would have more time for play. But mostly I ran to get out of the range of adults and thus escape reminders of uncompleted chores or errands to do.

In my early years, I usually was the only girl hanging around boys. We shared the same interests, but I envied them. Unlike me, they enjoyed unquestioned rights to own bikes, get balls for toys and never have to explain cuts and bruises harvested in hard physical play. I had a weird hair cut, dirty shorts, a body size that qualified me for a puppet show, and skin darkened by the scorching afternoon sun and devoid of the Vaseline most girls use to keep themselves soft. Vaseline wasn't a boy thing. My appearance gave me the camouflage I needed: I fooled the adults who occasionally walked past our gang of soccer-loving kids unaware that one of us was female There was only one test I didn't pass: I failed to piss while standing. I tried – I really did – but I failed at that.

As I entered my teenage years, I longed even more for the freedom boys had as a birthright – the freedom to dream beyond sleep of retracing the footsteps of legends like Pele. Boys had liberty and support that I lacked. To avoid falling forever behind them, I had to do something fast. So I lied. I shaved my head at the barber shack and chose baggy clothing instead of the dresses my siblings handed down to me in a constant and unwanted reminder of the limitations of my gender. I was certain that I, a by-product of my parents' passions and love, was meant to be a boy. What had gone wrong?

Along life's road, I found a special companion: a metallic cup. With a cream-colored layer of paint to cover her nakedness and flowers printed all over her body, she sat on the first shelf in the kitchen until a small opening at the bottom rendered her unfit for human use. Then, she was banished from the cupboard and sentenced to a life without service. I took her in and sheltered her from the shame that comes with the realization that one is useless. In time, she developed scars all over her body as my tough right foot lovingly sent her bouncing off the stones in the compound. I did all a girl could do to guard this prized possession from the prying eyes of my mother and the greedy grasp of the scrap collector. But he finally got her. I have never forgiven him for that.

Boys had better toys. Their first balls were made from banana fibers. As the years passed and industrialization hit their little brains, they improved on these toys, using breath blown into plastic milk packets to form the inner vacuums of balls and then wrapping them with miles of black rubber bands purchased from a local car mechanic. I longed to see how far my feet could send one of these wondrous orbs flying. I imagined my kicks exciting the screams of spectators. But those who owned the balls set the rules: They never let me play. I was four years older than they were because it had taken me time to gain the courage to oppose culture and pursue soccer. And to make matters worse, my game surely did stink; no one would risk defeat by adding me to his squad.

So most of the time I just sat and watched. My early playing years were spent standing at the ash-marked touch line, watching these little boys as they reminded me with each dribble, kick, pass and goal that soccer was tailor-made for males. This was no place for a girl, but I was engrossed. The only reliable reminder of time was the growing darkness that signaled all players it was time to go. I always got home late, and faced a beating because I couldn't explain where I had been the entire afternoon. Mama didn't help, but neither did she hurt me – at least not as much as these boys did by not letting me play.

Eventually, I sought other outlets for my energies. Swimming looked appealing; my few times at the pool were moments of celebration. But the joy didn't last long. I couldn't find a team, nor could I pay admission fees at a local swimming pool. Mama couldn't figure me out, so she sent me to my aunt's home, where I was confined behind a boundary wall with an opening that could only be operated by one who was way above the age of consent. This was prison to me, my confinement made all the more painful by the joyful noise of kids in the neighboring houses who had just the right numbers to play – and thus no need for the help of an outsider. Without sports, I had no hope. I choose silence. I decided to shut up and let the world – at least my aunt's world – move on without me. I choose to wait.

Fragments of freedom finally came in secondary school, when I was able to play basketball. Again, I was the only female student who spent recess playing sports with boys. My teachers defined me by the company I kept and my areas of interest. Some called me by my father's name. Others decided to wait until I grew out of my madness, certain that my biological clock finally would signal this game to an end. But at least I got to play.

The school didn't allow sports kits during the week or when it wasn't a sports term, so I played in my school uniform. My knee-length grey skirt had to endure rapid body movements without tear. My white blouse, which had to withstand the rough grips of guys who had failed to take the ball from me fairly, got torn. But my uniform's biggest job was to suck in all the sweat that my body produced as I ran up and down the court – a blend of raw salt I had been consuming every day, body fragrance, fluids that I took to keep my mother off my case, and anything else that I picked up as bodies met in the name of the game. By the end of each school day, my grey skirt was darker than everyone else's – especially the buttocks area. I always waited until it was dark, walked home and went straight into the bathroom. Thank God for younger siblings; Mama was too busy with them to notice me.

When I was 17, a neighbor told me about a girls' soccer team that had a game the next day. With overwhelming excitement, I borrowed a pair of men's boots. They were two sizes too large for me, but with them and years of training with the tin cup behind me, I finally played my first game. This breakthrough came with insults from the home crowd, foul play from a team that would beat us with their eyes shut and teammates whose names I didn't know. We lost 6-0. But despite the silence in the taxi ride back to Kampala and a few mumblings in search of what went wrong, I came home on top of the world. The sorrow that accompanies such a huge loss before a number of spectators was easily drowned by the fact that I had played a match with a real referee and in a jersey. We would surely win some other time.

I officially joined the team after my first game. It didn't take me long to discover that we were quite an unusual collection of talent. Any girl who would dare run after a rolling ball was admitted. The team was born of one man's desire to change society and its lack of support for female sports. My earliest teammates were netballers, volleyballers, aspiring cross country runners, two boxers, a basketball player, two teenagers, an up and coming artist, a traditional dancer and a mother. We were a perfect blend of broken dreams, undiscovered abilities, and prior disappointments, all united by a hunger for freedom and approval. We were athletes. Over the years, we have built a chain of support that is envied by many who gaze upon it from afar.

Where has all this left me? I have struggled with culture, family, self and failure. I have been labeled *kyakula sajja* – "grown like male" – a title awarded to those who desert the supposed glory of African womanhood. But, scarred and toughened by training and endless falls, we pick up a standard set by generations of women before us – to develop our God-given abilities, to pursue our once-forbidden dreams and at the same time to answer our culture's fears by showing that we still can honor and fulfill men's marital fantasies. We will never use our physical abilities to take away men's culturally-bestowed powers. We will bear them children despite our years of training. We will draw a clear line between soccer and lesbianism, and otherwise remain complete, African women.

As we make progress, my greatest disappointment remains coaches who seek personal benefits from the sweat of young female athletes – coaches who claim that most female athletes won't last long and who use that as a pretext to take away our rewards. I also resent fans who watch our games with only one intention: to find a healthy and fit woman to take home after the game. What a shame. Women's sport has lost much talent to such attitudes.

But change has become inevitable. Years after my first serious soccer competition I finally played under improved conditions, cheered on by fans who looked beyond tradition, wearing a jersey rather than borrowed clothes, and at last given a chance to prove myself worthy of trust and support.

Today, as a professional architect, I wish I were given an opportunity to start my youthful dreams anew – to meet the physical requirements, support my team with all I have, pass the ball, score and celebrate. I have accepted in my heart that I will never be a part of the team that celebrates victory on the pitch. My place once again is on the touch line as I cheer on those who have been given a chance to play for a greater audience and cause. But I will never abandon my dream. It's my sweet realization that a goal will be achieved if one faithfully passes on that which she thinks belongs to her.

The glories hung from athletes' necks are simply displays of obstacles cleared before the start of their races.

Memories of Rural Uganda

By Sophie Bamwoyeraki

It was 40 years ago, but I still remember the time Simba, my neighbor's dog, bit my sister. Some of my friends and I were outraged, so we set out to administer our brand of street justice. Armed with canes, we hunted the villain down, and soon trapped her between a large mango tree and an overgrown shrub. Each of us prepared to mete out five lashes to teach the creature a lesson it would never forget. But the poor dog's first yelp brought the ancient widow Sabina shuttling forth to deliver a stern lecture on kindness to animals. Downcast and ashamed, we grudgingly flung away our weapons. In the end, we were the ones who learned a lesson that day.

Such was life in Nyakaronko, the village in Western Uganda where I grew up in the early 1970s. Most parents in my village were semi-literate. While many looked to the religious institutions for guidance in child rearing and settling minor family wrangles, the real backbone of our upbringing was the community itself. It dictated our social roles, how we went about rituals like weddings and funerals, and how children should be raised. Among its cardinal rules: Anyone could discipline a child found doing wrong.

I miss those times. I miss walking in a village where everyone knew who I was and felt a responsibility to correct me when I erred. I yearn for the days when I had *omweeza*, first-fruit harvest lunches, with my brothers and their families. I fondly remember Christmas times, when "nightingales" would move from one home to another singing carols and receiving gifts and other tokens of appreciation. In fact, I long for all holidays, because that was when cousins filled our home. All guests had to be treated with our best hospitality, which sometimes meant giving up our meals, our cozy beds and even our clothing to make visitors feel welcome and comfortable. But our guests gave us something too. Most people came with *omushenga*, offerings ranging from newly harvested crops to calves or newly-made handcrafts like stools, baskets or mats. And they would be rewarded with something that matched what they had brought. If they had brought a calf, for instance, its first calf would be presented to them in the future.

All the aunts who visited, all the distant relatives who came over, all the old women and men who called on us had authority over us children. They watched whatever we did, how we did it and when we did it. It was our duty as children to listen to them and obey.

One's *tatenkazi*, or paternal aunt, had much more authority than any other person. Thank God, ours, Kezia, was friendly and not strict. My father had allocated to her a portion of his huge banana plantation. She was a regular visitor to our home, and when she came she usually brought already-made millet for us to eat. Her home was about four kilometers from ours, but she trudged the distance with steaming millet in a basket, balancing it on her head all the way. We, in turn, regularly went to visit her, carrying milk, newly harvested beans, roasted meat from a recently slaughtered calf, banana juice, milk and sugar. We each carried something on our heads. The journey, which most of us considered an adventure, would take at least two hours. When we arrived, Aunt Kezia would treat us to boiled maize and sparkling, fermented millet porridge. She always observed us, checking to see whether we knew how to cook, take care of our home and behave. She always took girls aside to whisper in our ears about being good wives. I was not really interested in such advice, but I showed respect and listened attentively. Whether I understood it or not, I knew my father's sister deserved as much respect as my father.

Respect for authority extended far beyond aunts. My father used to ask Balaam, our cousin who was then in a teacher-training college, to come to our home to give us lessons. A charismatic young man, he would wake us up at six in the morning with a bell, rather than the more customary rim of a tire. As soon as the gong went off, we would all dash out of our beds to wash and prepare for the day. We would hurry through breakfast consisting of milk, boiled maize, boiled *gonja* (plantain), bread, millet porridge, roasted groundnuts and boiled eggs. Then all dozen of us would parade in the compound. Balaam would stride among us conducting a health inspection – checking our fingernails, teeth and hair.

One morning, Clement, one of my big brothers, brought a small bottle of honey that had been harvested the previous evening. As Balaam was inspecting us, Clement put it to his mouth. But Balaam saw him and confiscated the bottle, hurling all the contents out. Buzzing bees flew in from all corners for a free feast as Clement sulked. But eventually he joined the rest of us in singing a chorus Balaam taught us.

> *Trust and obey for there is no other way*
> *To be happy in Jesus, but to trust and obey*

When I was young, I never thought about people having rights – even when conditions seemed unfair. I never questioned the clear distinction between girls' and boys' chores, for instance. Girls had to grow, weed and harvest crops; sweep family compounds; tend to the flower gardens; prepare meals and wash up after them; clean around the home; boil family bathing water and more. Our work prepared us for hard lives, and kept us close to home. Boys had it easier. They mostly looked after cows, sheep and goats in the field. Besides being less demanding, boys' work allowed them to roam, while girls had to stay close to home. Nobody could question this division of labor. It would be a source of mockery if a man was found in the kitchen peeling bananas, mingling millet or preparing a cup of tea.

Similarly, villagers would raise eyebrows if they found a girl riding a bicycle, whistling, climbing fruit trees or talking back to a man. Girls did have some moments of quiet satisfaction, though. I remember my brother had to go to a school away from our home to teach during his four-month A-Level (advanced secondary-school) vacation. The school assigned him a house, but since he had never done any house chores in his life, he was lost trying to prepare his meals. He resorted to steaming bananas in their covers. Luckily, some family friends came to his rescue by inviting him to their home for dinner every day.

Over time, I came to understand that girls' chores were home-based to protect us from assaults and attacks from strangers and malicious people. Indeed, everyone protected their children, and believed that other people's children behaved badly. Girls were never allowed to wander in the village; the only families I knew very well were within two kilometers of my home. I expected I would never get to know other children who were my age living in the same village but going to different schools.

Once I personally observed how dangerous life could be for girls. It was December, and all dozen of my parents' children were out of school. One day, I was part of a group assigned to help weed all the flower gardens and to clean the huge compound. Eager to finish chores as early as possible, we set off with a wheelbarrow, rake, hoe and broom as soon as we finished breakfast. By ten o'clock, as we returned to the main house, we heard screams of someone whose voice we recognized. Looking through the window, we saw a relative who was about 20 years old defiling a much younger girl who lived with us and worked as a helper around the home. I was just eight, and did not understand what they were doing. But even if I did, I was powerless to intervene. As a young girl, I could not just walk up to an elder and say I had witnessed a defiler in the act. That would besmirch his relatives.

Our upbringing, which taught us as children to be quiet and obedient, gave this defiler great freedom. Later when we had grown up, he shocked many by boasting that he had deflowered most of the helpers in the household. His bad character made many people hate and mistrust him even in his old age.

I don't think anyone living in our home would have gotten away with defilement. Both boys and girls were prohibited from hanging out with friends – "loitering," as father termed it. One evening, my brother Gregory thought he could take "French leave" to attend a disco dance after a neighbor's wedding. But as he stepped into the cold air for his unauthorized outing, our father, who was outside keeping watch, flashed his torch at him.

'Where are you going?' father bellowed from behind a huge tree that stood at the corner of the massive compound.

"Short... short call... I am going for a short call," Gregory stammered, rushing back inside the house without completing his supposed mission to relieve himself. Frightened, he slid into his bed fully dressed – shoes, trousers, shirt, tie, sweater, jacket and all. Then there was silence. Croaking frogs could be heard from a distance. The dog in the compound barked in reply to another one far off. But father came to the bed where Gregory now was safely tucked in.

"Get out of bed," Father hissed. Gregory pulled himself out of bed, bit by bit. "Do you always go to bed fully dressed, like this?"

"Ye... ye... yes...," Gregory stuttered.

Father gave him a long lecture, leaving him in tears. From then on, the front door was locked every night and a heavy couch was placed against it. If anyone tried to move it, they would be heard from our parents' bedroom.

That marked the end of anyone attempting to go to village discos. The impact was long-lasting. To this day, I do not feel drawn to socializing or adventure travelling.

Some temptations are impossible to resist, though. Once, a relative visited and asked us to recite our rhymes. Impressed with our proficiency in English (he must have ignored most of the words that we garbled), he rewarded us handsomely with coins. Straightaway I headed for a neighboring village that was well-known for growing succulent sugarcane. One of my elder brothers had pointed out the house where I could buy the sweet snack; I could see it clearly from our home, which was built on a hill. I thought that I would get there quickly, but my young eyes misjudged the distance. Hours later, I returned home empty-handed. Covered in dust and disappointed, I immediately encountered Father in his favorite place, waiting for my return. I greeted him quickly, hurried through the explanation of my misadventure, and rushed inside to heap rags on my backside in preparation for the punishment I was sure would befall me. To my surprise, my well-padded back escaped harm. The beating never came. And the next day, my father brought us sugarcanes he picked up on his way home from work.

Yes, I was blessed with a loving father who protected me from the harsher realities of my community. Many grown women were less lucky. Despite all the work they did and all the time they spent tending to children, women were never consulted on important decisions concerning child rearing. Society had a saying that the dullest of men is a better discussant than the brightest of women. Men's decisions were final.

That was not the worst of it. Women commonly suffered violence from drunken, negligent and abusive husbands. But by the age of twelve, I knew that divorce was not an option in our culture. Only in rare cases could a man return his wife to her parents. If he did, he would demand a refund of the bride wealth that he had given to her parents. The bride's brothers used this wealth to give presents to the parents of their own wives. Every girl was brought up knowing well that she was going to fetch bride wealth for her family. Whenever anyone even uttered the word "divorce" all the mothers crossed their hearts.

While divorce was unthinkable, for some women marriage was unbearable, as I learned firsthand. In the seventies, life was hard. Nora dropped out of school at the age of 15 to get married as second wife to Senta, a man whose first wife had borne girls only. Nora had to till the ground to feed her children. And as the Creator could have it, in nine years she bestowed on Senta the honor that the first wife had denied him: six sons. Nora worked very hard. The piece of land Senta had given her was too small to support her. She got by in part because my family gave her odd jobs from which she earned a few shillings and sometimes a bunch of *matooke* or one or two kilograms of sweet potatoes. But her husband sweet-talked her into surrendering to him all her monetary income, which he used not to buy new seeds for planting or food for the six sons who received education only up to primary three. No, he used it to buy *waragi*, a potent, locally-brewed gin made from bananas. Disappointed and desperate, Nora would complain, but Senta rained beatings on her until she would run out of the house to spend a night in the latrine or in the makeshift kitchen.

One cold evening, mother prepared a large kettle of tea and asked me to put butter on many slices of bread because we were to have visitors. Nora and her husband were coming for a reconciliation meeting. After a night of beatings, Nora had fled to her parents, but now her husband wanted her back. When I asked why Nora had to put up with such a spouse, Mother simply said no one should ever consider divorce. I could not understand, and I told Mum that if a man beat me like that I would beat him up too. She shuddered.

Later, I could hear the deliberations from my bedroom.

"I'm very sorry about my conduct," Senta apologized. "I am ashamed of what I did, and I shall treat you well, if you return."

"You have said this before," Nora murmured, "and I don't think you will change at all."

The elders in the meeting acted as if they had not heard what she said. They gave her a lecture on how to be a better wife. A team of youths were dispatched to pick up her suitcase from her parents' home. A few weeks later, the violence resumed. It became routine in her life.

Perhaps the story of Nora helped me understand a bit the tragic story of Muhooza's mother. She was in a polygamous marriage, as were most families. We were often told that such families got on well, but the reverse was true. Her son had completed school with brilliant results. He told us he wanted to study to become a doctor. We all laughed at him because we thought he would be cleaning patients' wounds and giving injections – work that seemed a lot less appealing to us than becoming lawyers, teachers or secretaries. His mother felt the sting of the taunts we aimed at her son. One day, she invited one of her son's tormenters, his stepbrother, over to her house for a meal. She gave them drinks, and then returned to the kitchen to bring the main meal. Out of her sight, Muhooza exchanged his calabash with his stepbrother's, which was smaller. He guzzled his stolen drink in a second. By the time his mother returned, Muhooza was foaming at the mouth and grunting like a pig. Within three hours his soul had departed from his still body. Muhooza's stepbrother narrated what had happened, but there was insufficient evidence for police to prosecute Muhooza's mother. After a family meeting, she was banished from the village for fear that she might kill more people.

By the 1980's, our family had one of the leading homes in the village. Our father, who travelled widely across the district, emulated the excellent practices he came across. Our farm was clean and organized. We won sub-county agriculture competitions. Thanks in part to the influence of relatives who lived in the capital city, the children all were educated. Our parents tried to influence us to take interest in farming, but none of us was interested.

I left my home district in the 1980's to study at university. I got married in 1983, and have lived in Kampala ever since. Living in the capital city is a great advantage. For one thing, my husband and I were able to send our children to very good schools all the way from primary school to university. Whereas my parents had 12 children, my husband and I decided to have only four so as to be able to educate them fully. Our plan is to ensure that each one of them attains postgraduate education before reaching age 30. We are doing our best to get them as well-qualified as possible so that they can contend successfully in this competitive world.

Slowly, our society is fixing what was horrendous about it. We are educating all our children, and sensitizing women about their rights. Many now are reporting domestic violence, and defilement is starting to earn men prison sentences. Many young, educated men are shunning polygamy, viewing it as an economic burden.

And yet sometimes, despite our success, I feel sad. We have lost something.

Our children, who went to "modern" schools, all learned English as their first language. A few years ago, our son, who went to a university in our home region to study medicine, actually had to take language classes to master his own mother tongue so he could communicate with semi-literate patients. And while my extended family now boasts many graduates – doctors, engineers, lawyers and teachers – we have lost touch with many of them. Like us, many in our extended family have become more focused on the nuclear family. They "mind their own business." They do not feel obliged to address or discipline children who are not their own.

Other things have changed too. Gone are the days when homes were filled with cousins spending holidays together. While first cousins still know each other well, second cousins feel they are not related at all. They barely know each other. We meet at weddings, funerals and sometimes at graduation parties. And while my husband and I regularly send our daughter to the village where I was born to master the language, learn to cook local food and mix with the people, it's not the same.

For instance, my daughter never heard the folk stories that I learned from our visiting cousins. I remember listening to my cousin, Namatovu, tell us story after story after dinner until we all fell asleep around her. Her stories taught us many things, such as the importance of not rushing into marriage simply because a suitor is handsome and rich. I particularly remember the story about the ogre that used to eat people.

The ogre disguised himself as a flawless, tall, handsome man. Once he met a girl who fell in love with him. Within one month, the girl introduced him to her parents. The parents did not need a lot of convincing because he had imprisoned their ability to reason by giving them expensive gifts such as cattle and goats. He even built a modern house for them, and bought them lots of clothes. The wedding preparations, which normally take about two years, were rushed, and few questions were asked about his immediate family. The wedding party cost him a fortune, leaving everyone in the girl's village smacking their lips in wonder. After a year, the couple had a baby girl, but the child disappeared after her first birthday. All the searches were in vain; the child was gone, and was soon forgotten. Again, the couple had a baby, and this one also disappeared after her first birthday. As before, all the searches were in vain. The third-born was a boy. The mother hoped he would not suffer the same fate as her earlier babies. She went everywhere with him strapped on her back, and could only place him down when they all went to sleep. Sometimes, she would jump out of her sleep crying and looking for him only to find him in his cot. Eventually, she decided to remain awake at night to guard her child. When the boy was one year old, her fears grew worse. One night, as she was keeping watch, she heard her husband get up. He picked up the baby from his cot. She sat up in bed, and watched him go out of the bedroom. Standing on trembling legs, she threw a kikoyi (shawl) on her shoulders and followed. He walked more than two kilometers to caves that people in the village always feared to enter. He went in, and she followed. In the dim light from a magical lamp, she recognized her two girl children and about a score other children. The children had turned into beings that were half human, half snake. She screamed, and called her children's names. Her husband threw the baby boy down, and instantly turned into a snake and swallowed her up.

Such stories made us careful about what we did. We believed them to be true until we grew up.

I long for the times when I, as a university student, followed my cousin's footsteps, sitting down with my nieces and nephews to read to them. Their favorite stories came from *African Myths and Legends* retold by Kathleen Arnott. I am sure they learned many moral lessons from these fables.

Recently, when I returned home for a visit, I was impressed to discover that almost all the children in the village now were going to school, and fewer girls were dropping out of school to get married. But I must admit I was sad, too, for the lost chance to help them. They no longer need someone to read to them.

A lot has changed, but memories of the old times are still precious.

A Victim No More

By Grace Namazzi*

I remember as if it were yesterday riding on the back of a bicycle as we travelled the 32 kilometers from Lukaya, a small town on the Kampala-Masaka highway, to my village in Maguluka. But it actually was two decades ago. I was about seven years old.

My mother, a struggling single mother, could barely keep her life together. She had no education, having dropped out of school after her father's death. She had reached the big city hoping for a better life, but the city had ideas of its own. She was unable to support herself, so she lived with relatives. Then she fell in love and got pregnant with me. She was only 20 years old. The twins, my sister and brother, came soon after me. She tells how she used to walk along the railroad in search of milk, with one child on her back, one on her front and another (me) tugging at her dress. She sold charcoal at a street corner to raise money to put food on the table. My sister died at four months when the twins were infected with pneumonia. You can still read the pain on my mother's face on the rare occasions she brings up the subject. My dad? Well, his beer mattered more to him than the mother of his children.

---

* Not the author's real name

Desperate, my mother sent me to live with my grandmother in the village for almost three years while she cared for the sick boy. I remember the dreadful walks to school in the village. I would wake up, and jump into my school uniform without taking a bath. I was one of the few kids lucky enough to be able to buy a uniform and books. My grandmother couldn't afford shoes or socks, though, and even if my mum sent these from the big city, my grandmother made me save them for Christmas or in case we had to go to town. Sometimes, when Christmas came, they no longer fit.

After getting dressed, I would rush to the kitchen, and get the leftover food from the previous night's meal. This would be my lunch, which I would eat cold a few hours later. The tiring walk to school seemed endless. I wanted to go back and dream in the warmth of my bed. The stones and thorns pricking my little feet made matters worse. So did the jiggers eating into my skin. I hated getting to school too, because the bigger girls would take away my lunch or mat. How I wished my mum could visit from the big city, if not to take me with her, then at least to bring me new clothes and shoes that I could show off.

One day, God answered my prayers, and Mum came for me. But life continued to be hard for her. So even after I returned to live with her, my brother and I had to go to the village every school holiday. I always hated going back to the village. It meant that I wouldn't be under the protection of my dear mother. It meant missing city luxuries – television, light from bulbs, and my favorite cartoon, *Pingu*, which I watched at our neighbors' home. It meant that I would spend sleepless nights scratching and shooing off fleas that would feed on my blood while everyone else snored. Holiday in the village also meant walking five miles down the hill to collect water in jerry cans, and then trudging back up the hill with it, thorns pricking my bare feet.

But most of all I hated the village for the ridicule I would face when I was away from mother. My self-esteem hit rock bottom, and I became so timid I even had to be careful how I took my steps so they would not disturb a certain auntie whose favorite pastime was to treat children with bitterness and bile. She loved putting us down, beating us at the slightest mistake or sending us to bed without food. When she walked into the compound we would scatter into the banana plantation. If we came back with jackfruit, she punished us for climbing the tree, but then would take our fruit and only let us have some if we were good to her.

So there I was, only nine years old, on a nearly broken-down bike slowly rattling down the rugged, dusty roads of Kalungu deep into the village where I would spend two months on holiday. I had made the trip before, but I nevertheless was near tears. I had no say in the matter, though. When Mum said I had to go, I had to go.

This particular holiday would be different.

One day not long after I arrived found me moping in the compound of an old house that belonged to my grandfather. After my morning work digging in the garden, I often would sit under a banana tree scratching my hands and wishing my mum would send for me. I would listen to the giggles of my cousins enjoying a game of hopscotch nearby. Our clothes were always in tatters; my grandmother believed that the clean clothes we had brought were meant for town, so she made us get by with just two dresses each for the entire holiday.

Other children sometimes ridiculed me for sitting there feeling sorry for myself. As the days passed and my mother didn't come for me, I started to accept my fate and slowly joined the other children. We were mischievous to a fault. We would go harvesting corn from people's gardens without permission, or climb mango trees and pluck their fruit, whether raw or ripe. I learned to climb trees, play football and throw a punch like a boy. My muscles started to tighten from all the exercise and doing things the boys' way.

I still spent a lot of time by myself lost in my thoughts, though. That's what I was doing this particular day – a day now seared in my memory. As I sat, my younger cousin ran over to me, and said our elder cousin needed me immediately. His father and my mother were half siblings. He was about seventeen. As the younger child, I was obliged to obey older children and do whatever they told me to do; in fact, younger children addressed older ones as *baaba*, an expression of respect. So I got up, and went off to honor my cousin's call. I was wearing my yellow school uniform from Kampala. I kicked a pebble as I made my way through the well-mulched banana plantation. We had been pruning the banana trees, and the garden looked clean.

When I approached the corn field, I noticed my cousin was amid the plants already picking his own corn. I didn't stop to wonder why he needed me since he could do the work himself; children were not allowed to question the actions of elders, even if they were beating us and we couldn't bear the pain.

It was nearing the end of harvest season. I can still see the dry corn sticks weathering away. There were a few ears of corn dotting the garden. We occasionally harvested them for breakfast or evening snack.

My cousin summoned me and I rushed to get to him. He asked me what I had been doing. He obviously knew because he had sent for me, but again it was not my place to question authority. So I replied that I was playing. I thought he was going to scold me. But he was nice, asking if I was fine. He picked an ear of corn and handed it to me. It was very rare for an older child to be nice to a younger one. We younger kids had to earn every favor. I was about to pay for mine.

He ordered me to take off my pants and pee. I followed his order without asking. But before I could get up, he told me to lie down without putting my pants back on and spread my legs. I didn't know what was happening, but I didn't have permission or the drive to question his order because that would earn me a beating. Then he got on top of me. I didn't know what was going on. I didn't blink, didn't ask questions. Nor did I resist.

In a matter of minutes I felt something running down my thighs. He then handed me a new handkerchief. I wondered why he was giving me a gift. But he told me to use it to clean myself, and then put on my pants.

I still remember the sound of a bell as a biker rode passed. I saw my cousin duck under the bushes, and my mind wondered why he was hiding. He looked at me, and whispered that I should stay quiet. I could see the bicyclist ride past the plantation and disappear. My cousin then got up, and told me not to tell anyone what had just happened. I didn't know what had happened, so what would I say anyway? And who would listen to me? I even feared telling elders that I had a thorn stuck in my foot or that I was thirsty because I might be accused of being careless or a nuisance. How would I tell anyone something I didn't even understand?

My cousin rewarded me with some of the best corn he had harvested, and sent me on my way. I went back to play with the other kids. But when I reached them, I felt uncomfortable, and decided just to sit and watch.

I returned to Kampala two months later, but trouble soon followed me. My mother had secured a job as a chef for the students at a technical school. It paid enough for a one-room house. It was in a slum, but it at least gave her some control over her life. Better still, she could carry home leftover food or buy food at cheaper prices from the school's bulk purchase.

Being a member of an extended family, she started taking in some cousins whose parents had died. As fate would have it, the two children she took in were my cousin the abuser and his sister. All five of us – my mother and four children – lived in that single room.

Soon, my torment began again.

My mother was very unhappy with so many children to take care of and little income to cover our many needs. This ate away at her spirit, turning her into a tough woman. She never tolerated nonsense. We had to be on our best behavior. She came home every day very tired, and went straight to bed. Because she had not attained an education, she did not spend time helping us with our homework. We never even talked much because she was either at work or resting. I always promised myself that when I had my own children I would throw them in the air and catch them, swing them around and just laugh with them. I would talk and talk, and ask them to tell me everything. I vowed to love them the way I saw the white people do in the movies.

When my cousin came to live with us, he acted as if he had been handed a free card to have sex with me at will. And he used that card over and over and over again. He used it as a punishment for everything I did wrong. If he sent me to the shops and thought I had taken too long, he would punish me in his unique way. If I did something that my mother had warned me against, he threatened to report me if I refused to let him do as he pleased.

As I grew up, I slowly realized that what he was doing was wrong. The movies said so. I saw other kids get punished for experimenting with sex. But when I started showing signs of resistance towards him, he resorted to threats. If I so much as looked out of the compound with the idea of going and playing, he promised that he would report me to my mother. Only if I let him do what he wanted would he let me go play with other kids.

He also said that even if I told my mother, she wouldn't believe me, pointing out a few times that she had not believed me even when I was telling the truth. He told me my mother didn't love me.

I believed him. I had no place to run, and he continued to defile me at will. I retreated into my own world, sometimes spending hours on end staring at people. I imagined they wouldn't miss me if I disappeared. My tormentor had told me that nobody, not even my dear mum, would care.

When I went to boarding school, I often curled up in a ball and listened as the other girls talked about their cousins with pride. Later, in high school, I always kept still when other girls would talk about their first experiences with sex. I developed teenage crushes on cute boys, but was too afraid to associate with them because I felt I was unworthy of their time. Nothing would make me engage in sex.

When I went to college in 2001, I was required to go for a medical check-up. I froze because I knew they were going to ask me for an HIV test. Every fiber in my body screamed that I had AIDS. I had been battling an itch down there for years, but I feared telling anyone because I thought they would ask me how I got it.

When the test was done, I was given some drugs to take home. I thought they were antiretrovirals. Certain I had AIDS, I hid the pills from my mum, and worried myself to sleep for weeks. I spent days pondering every little memory I could collect of those days back in the village. I was going to die. I was going to die in shame.

That itch all those years stopped with that one course of medication. But I paid a price. When I finally asked my friend whose mother was a nurse to find out what this particular drug treated, the answer came back: gonorrhea. Her mother didn't want her to associate with me again because she believed I would spoil her daughter.

Eventually, we moved to a house with two rooms because my mother took in another late uncle's wife after he suddenly passed on. The woman was pregnant with her first child who would never see his father.

My cousin never did housework because he was a man. In traditional settings, boys and men do not do any housework. They only dig, collect water and chop firewood. Girls are brought up to take care of men. Sisters must do their brothers' laundry, even if the sisters are older. This is meant to prepare them to be good, caring, hardworking and submissive wives. So while we washed, cleaned the house and cooked, my cousin stayed in bedroom watching TV and scratching his balls. There was no firewood to chop in the town, nor any garden to till, and tap water was so near that we children also had the job of fetching it.

One day, I finally decided I had had enough. I couldn't take it anymore. The breakthrough came on a day when I found my cousin with his hand inside his pants as he watched TV. I had been sent in to collect a bar of soap. He told me to go outside and call his sister, who was nineteen. When I found her, she told me to go back and tell him she was busy and couldn't go. I returned to my waiting cousin, and conveyed her message. He told me to remind her that he would report her for the things she had done if she didn't go straight into the bedroom. She still refused. That is when I realized that he was not defiling only me. She was also his victim. His sister. But she had said no. She had turned him down, and he didn't hit her. She didn't care whether he told on her. She just didn't give into his demands.

I realized that I could say no too, that I could refuse and there would be nothing he could do. When his sister refused him, he turned to me, and said I should go closer to where he was lying. I said no. He asked if I knew what was good for me. I looked down at my dress, played with imaginary thread, put on an angry face and stood firm. "No." I didn't care anymore how much trouble this could bring me. I finally knew that what was going on was wrong. I didn't care if my mother would punish me for it. I just didn't want it to go on anymore. My cousin became very cold towards me, but I didn't care. After all, I wasn't the only one who would be in trouble with him. I wasn't the only one rejecting his advances.

My mother never got to know what was happening. I never told. I didn't know how she would take it. But when I grew up I learned that I actually could have been saved from all those years of anguish if I had opened up to one person – my grand-mother.

I should have known. Of all sins, messing around with boys was the gravest any girl could commit in her house. I learned this one day when my grandmother caught one of my aunties red-handed with a man in the plantations at night. The screaming and beatings woke us up. My auntie got beaten badly for days on end. She stayed in her room for weeks. She was not allowed to eat with the rest of us. For days, my grandmother went out, got drunk, and came back home to lash her, using every insult in the book. And when she learned that the man she had caught with her daughter was much older, she went to the local council chairman and reported his crime.

They didn't arrest the man, but she went back countless times, sometimes enlisting help from friends. When the local council leader didn't help, she got angry and turned to higher-ranking officials. The man was summoned, and recorded a statement. When he was sent home (my grandmother believed he had bribed the local council leaders to set him free), she went to the police and reported again. The man was arrested, but later released. She sold some of her harvest, collected money and jumped on a bike to the district headquarters to report the matter there. They promised to get back to her, but they never did. She implored relatives who lived in Kampala to help.

The man was not put away for good. To this day, my grandmother has never forgiven her local leaders or the relatives who ignored her pleas for help.

Imagine what she would have done to my cousin had I confided in her. She might have saved me the abuse all those years. But I never gathered the courage to tell her or my mother. I couldn't put them through such emotional torture and pain. Unless my uneducated mum and grandmother read this, they will never know.

The abuse didn't just take away my innocence and childhood. For years, it left me questioning my own worth. I lived in doubt of my mother's love towards me. Until adulthood, I didn't share anything with her. I didn't bother asking for any favors because I imagined she would automatically say no or that she would scold me. I had been made to believe that she didn't really care about me. I only realized otherwise when I was well into my 20s. I had to find a way out of that agony. I was not going to live the rest of my life based on a past that I couldn't change.

I haven't seen my cousin since he left home when I was still a child. I keep hoping that he is dead, because I do not have the energy to ask after him.

I know that there are many women like me who have gone through abuse by close relatives – uncles, cousins, older brothers, neighbors, family friends, even fathers. I know many girls suffer the same abuse at the hand of pedophiles who coerce them with threats and sometimes enjoy the support of families eager to keep the defilement under wraps to protect their names. I know such girls suffer in silence. Other victims do not know where to seek help, and sometimes by the time they finally do, their abusers have destroyed evidence. Many children continue to be humiliated, as their parents prefer to settle matters by collecting payments from offenders out of court.

More girls prefer to keep quiet, to go on to get married and live "normal" lives, with no one to remind them that they are victims of unspeakable abuse.

But I chose to break free – free of fear and shame. I believe I have done a damn good job.

The Girl with Scars

By Hilda Twongyeirwe

Now they no longer bother me, but when I was younger, my scars were an issue. To hide them, I learned to wear trousers in a village where girls who wore trousers were dismissed as "girls who were men." People who criticized me did not know that I wore trousers mainly to cover my scars, and to avoid the questions that always came my way. *Ehh, mwishiki okabaki amaguru*, they would say. "What happened to your legs?"

As a young woman, I used to love acting in stage plays. Once, after acting in a college music and drama festival, I sat in the audience as the results were announced. I was thrilled when I heard my name announced as the best actress of the year. But then I heard some boys who were seated in front of me. "The girl with scars has taken the best actress trophy," one said. My heart sank. Instead of celebrating my win, I found myself asking God questions that he had no obligation to answer. But I learned a lesson. Since that time, I do not describe people by their defects.

The story of my legs began when I was about to sit for my Primary Leaving Examinations (PLE). I woke up one day with an itch on my left leg. I scratched it, but then it started feeling sore. My mother told me not to scratch. *Iwe nooza kwehutaaza obuwayeyagura okashusha ngu okuguru neibaare,* she said. "You will hurt yourself scratching as if your skin is made out of stone." My mother was in a class of her own. She never battered us the way we saw some mothers hit their children. Some women in our village said she spoiled us by not beating us. But in reality, mother was both firm and gentle at the same time.

After she left the room, I scratched some more. My brother teased, "Just scratch until you see blood. Jane (our mother) does not know the kind of itch underneath your skin." My brother and I were tight friends. We spent most of our time together – fetching water, helping mother clean the green compound, fetching firewood and washing utensils. We also walked together to the gardens to collect potatoes, fresh peas, beans and Irish potatoes. I cherished the times he chased boys who disturbed and teased me. He was my keeper for all the years I had him.

After the scratching, we headed for school. It took us only about five minutes to dash from home, cross the small stream on the school road and reach the school gate. Kacerere Primary is tucked away close to the Uganda-Rwanda boarder in the undulating hills of Kabale. We used to sing a popular song in praise of our school.

> *Stand on top of the hills*
> *Up above there*
> *Look at what lies below you.*
> *There is a magnificent school*
> *That is called Kacerere Primary School.*
> *Oh Kacerere, you are beautiful*
> *You are stunning*
> *Indeed you are gorgeous.*
> *All of us, young and old,*
> *Let's say, "KACERERE!"*

By evening, my leg was swollen. The itch had developed into a boil. By the end of week, another boil had come up on my other leg. From then on, boils started competing for space on my legs, sometimes leaving scars. The boils attacked the same part on both legs – the nice part that gets exposed when a woman sits cross legged. I went to village clinics, but the boils kept coming relentlessly. My grandmother smeared herbs, but nothing changed. Every so often my brother and his friends had to support me as I walked home because I would be in so much pain I could not walk on my own.

As soon as I completed my exams, my mother led me to her sister, whose husband worked in a government hospital. They both took me to doctors who gave me medicine, but nothing changed. The doctors never gave any explanation why the medicine did not work. Whenever I would see them, they would look at the papers and change the treatment. But the boils kept coming, bringing more pain with them. I can still feel that pain. It took my whole body hostage. And then people would ask, "What are these? What happened? How do they come? Do they pain you? What medicine do you use? Why don't you go to hospital? Maybe you ate a mysterious something." Maybe this…Maybe that…Maybe….

As weeks turned into months and months into years, a deep fear began to grow in me. Doctors would hold my legs and say nothing. I began to wonder what they were thinking. I started to weave stories I imagined were in their mouths. I kept to myself most of the time because I felt very unlucky. I did not want the jolly and jumpy girls to fall on my hurting legs anyway.

People brought drugs and herbs they thought could cure me. One time, a friend of my father visited, and said I was suffering from "*enjobe.*" He said that he had seen other people with the same disease, and that they had got cured by rubbing the dry skin of an animal called *enjobe* on the affected areas.

Skin of an animal? That is witchcraft, I protested. I did not want anything to do with witchcraft because we grew up hearing that witchcraft was bad. Witchcraft is based on magic. Herbalists, on the other hand, are more acceptable because they use a scientific approach.

The man said that he had seen a son of our reverend take this treatment. "If you think that is witchcraft, it is not," he insisted. Later, he came with the reverend. They brought a piece of the dried skin of *enjobe* and rubbed it on both of my legs. The good reverend explained that the skin had medicinal properties that would enter my skin and cure the allergy that was bringing the boils. "How long do I have to do this?" I asked. "Maybe only two or three days," he said. "That should be enough, and you will be healed." After administering the skin treatment, he prayed, asking God for healing.

I threw away my pride and rubbed the skin on my legs, not just for two or three days but for more than a week. By the end of week, though, there was no change. I abandoned the skin and started going back to the village clinics for my injections, painkillers and dressing. I had constant fevers as a result of the boils.

After Senior Four (my fourth year of secondary school), I joined another school that was farther away from home, in another district. My leg problem was still with me. Sometimes I would get a few months without new boils, but then they returned. They seemed to come and go as they wished. In my new school, we used to fetch water from about a kilometer away. Many times I couldn't go to the well because of my swollen legs. A girl named Yvonne used to borrow the cook's bicycle and ride it to the well, returning with two cans of water. Sometimes she would give me one of the cans.

My boils were an advantage sometimes. When gardening time came, the teachers would leave me at school for fear I would get new infections. I enjoyed that, although I became lonely. But of course, during the good spells I would join the rest of the students to plant or harvest school food. We liked harvesting sweet potatoes especially because we would eat them to soothe our hunger.

At the end of senior five, I visited a young couple whom my father knew. Unfortunately, while I was there, a boil spell came. I could not go home as was planned. I stayed with them for more than two weeks. They were very kind. They had a visitor. As it's said in my language, *Obusaasi obutakurekire, obugambiraga otabukuburize.* "The pain that does not leave you alone makes you narrate it to a person who has not asked you about it." Somehow I found myself narrating my pain to this stranger. He listened, touching and turning the legs. At the end of my narration, he said that he knew an herbalist who could treat me. "He has healed many. I know him very well. This condition is nothing for his hands."

The couple, their visitor and I set off very early the next morning so that we would arrive with the sunrise. "He does not treat patients after the sun is high in the sky," the man said, "because during the day he is too busy searching bushes for new herbs. Also he says that medicine should be given in the morning."

When we reached the herbalist, he touched my legs and declared it was a simple disease. "In one week you should be okay. This is nothing compared to other ailments I have treated." He gave me some herbs to smear on my legs and others to drink. He gave me instructions written on a small piece of paper. The men paid him. I thanked them, and promised to use the herbs as he had instructed.

When I recounted the story to my mother, she was sad about the life that I had, but said she hoped the man's herbs would work. By the end of holiday, however, there was no change. I was now resigned, and I told my parents that I would not take any more herbs. They understood my frustrations, and never mentioned herbs again.

After senior six I was seated at home when my cousin Eunice visited. She told me that she knew a witch doctor who could return the boils to the person who sent them to me. I told her that she was mad. She laughed, and said she was just teasing. "This is a good woman herbalist. Do you remember when Rucogoza fractured both his legs? It was this woman who set his bones back to normal. Doctors had failed. Try her. She might be able to help." I told Eunice that I did not want anything more to do with herbalists. "Try one last time," she begged.

As soon as my mother came home that evening, she encouraged me to try one last time. *Ebya Ruhanga tomanya,* she said. "God's ways are not man's ways." My mother always told us to be positive, and not to give up. Mother gave birth to nine of us, and she cared and worried about all of us in equal measure. She died of high blood pressure at the age of 67. It is not the same when you have only one or two children to mind. When I was at her bedside in Mulago Hospital watching her breathe her last, I felt very proud to have been her daughter. Even as I held her hand and saw that she was gone, I felt a glow in my heart. I could never have chosen another mother for anything in the world.

When Dad came home for the weekend, mother told him about the woman herbalist. Those days we did not live with Dad regularly. He worked for local government, and had to move from place to place. Sometimes we would be with him, and other times we would be home in our village. "It is not a witch doctor you are talking about?" Dad inquired. He did not want anything to do with witchcraft. He often talked about how his father, after converting to Christianity, told all his children never to go into the ways of witchcraft. He explained to us that witch doctors were dangerous because they used magic and mystery, and pretended to have powers they did not have. They also stole from people by asking for a lot of money for services that never worked except by chance. He called them liars and cheats. Herbalists, on the other hand, were divine. They knew the medicine, and they charged very little because they took their knowledge as a blessing from God to help other people. Also, herbs are a gift of nature and so must not be traded. The fee for herbalists is called *obuteera kishaka*, literally meaning "token fee" to the person who goes into the bush to find the herbs. It was never payment for the herbs. After he was satisfied that the woman was not a witchdoctor, my father agreed to take the journey.

The following morning I woke before sunrise and we journeyed towards Lake Bunyonyi. Sunrise was becoming my motif – to kill me or save me, I thought as I watched day break. We had to walk because no public transport vehicles operated in that area. As daylight flooded the footpath, I hurried behind Dad. He was wearing his checkered coat and gray trousers. His back was straight and strong. His height lent him a bounce that came with each step that he took. I was proud of him. I still am, but in a different way. These days he is frail and weak most of the time. He is 77 as I write this story. His bounce has given way to a gentle stoop.

When I was younger, I did not realize the influence my dad had on me. It was after I started working and got married that I found myself referring to Dad many times in different situations. He was a special father to us and a special husband to my mother. I grew up listening to my friends' stories of domestic violence, but we never saw Dad fight mother. They shared a close relationship. The minute Mother passed away in hospital, my father telephoned me to ask how she was. He said that suddenly his spirit got shaky as if she was not well. When I told him she had just breathed her last, he simply said, *Aza oyehangane mwana wangye.* "I felt it. Be brave my child."

After we got into the canoe and the owner rowed away into the middle of the large lake, fear gripped me. We were surrounded by so much water, and the ripples tapped on the sides of the canoe continuously. "These days the lake is not very gentle," the canoe owner said. "But we shall cross. And if we die, it will be our day." I did not like the way he talked about death as if it was of no significance. I did not want this to be my day. Like a dangerous snake, the water meandered, its arms disappearing in between hills and emerging from behind other hills. It was as if the water was following us and marking our movements. Though frightening, it was beautiful. In the sunrise, the sky reflected in the lake was broken into shiny rivulets. It felt like a marriage between the water and the sky – like a promise that we were going be safe in between the two.

But the ripples increased and some water spilled into the canoe. I shivered and pulled the blue sweater I had borrowed from my mother around me. The canoe man told me not to shiver and not to worry about the little water that was escaping with the wind. "It is nothing compared to the water underneath the canoe," he said. Dad later told me the lake men appease the water by telling it that it is abundant. When the ripples increased, I called out to Dad and told him that we were making a mistake.

"Why?" he asked.

"Because we can drown in this lake for no reason at all," I replied.

"That is not true my child," he said. "We have a reason. Your healing is the reason we are on this journey."

Dad was seated behind me so I do not know the expression that my words brought to his face. But when he responded, I felt something stir my spirit. I was touched by the calm in his voice and the depth in his words. Then I knew that God would not let us drown in this lake. My father's words reached deep inside me and brought a new me to the surface – a stronger me. They brought out a girl ready to travel and return home whole. Since we were in a canoe, no one saw the tears that escaped my eyes. A serene aura descended on me, and I felt it settle above the canoe. We were safe. Maybe that is when I was healed.

Across the lake, we found people who directed us to the home of the woman we were seeking. When we got there, we found her seated outside. A few patients sat in the compound.

We went straight to her, but she told us that she would attend to me later. When my father tried to explain that we had come from far and that we would have wanted to go back early, she did not budge. "So you want me to leave what I am doing in order to do your biding?" she said. "Sorry but you just have to wait." She was busy weaving a cast for a man who had a back ailment. She did not even look at my legs. We had to wait.

It was almost evening when the woman called me to where she sat. My father had taken a walk after sitting for too long. She asked me a few questions, including whether I had ever sought the white man's medication. I responded to all her questions. Then she said she would heal me. This is not a disease for the hospital, she said. This type of boil is healed by herbs. She refused to explain what type of boil they were. She said it was not important. "What you want is to be healed, and I will heal you."

I did not want to hear the word "heal." I had heard it so many times before that it had become meaningless to me. Healing would come if it wanted to come, or refuse if it wanted to refuse.

"Where is your father, my child?"

"He is around," I said.

"Will he pay for my services?"

"Yes, he will." I did not want her to call me her child. I wanted her medicine, but nothing else to do with her.

Looking at the number of sick people in her compound disoriented me. This woman seemed to symbolize sickness and disease. My stomach was a knot that I could not untangle. It was as if an invisible hand had taken my stomach hostage, and was stirring everything in a steady and continuous motion, faster with each round. "When your father returns," she called out, "just tell him to pay what he can afford. You have suffered far too long." I nodded. I did not trust my voice to respond. It was too thin with emotion. The woman mixed herbs in a calabash, and smeared them on my legs. She mixed another set and gave them to me to drink. I hesitated. "Hold it and drink," she said. "What you people do not know is that the white man's medicine is extracted from our herbs. That is why they are potent." I took the calabash, and gulped down the green liquid. My tongue tingled.

Dad did not take long to return. He paid the woman, and she gave us more herbs to smear on the legs for three more days. We embarked on our journey home when it was almost dark, and we arrived late in the night. I was spent. We found mother still awake, waiting for us.

About a week later all the wounds had dried and no new boils came. For many months I waited for new ones to sprout but they did not.

Today the scars remain, but with the passage of time the feeling is different. I do not think about the scars, even when I decide to wear a mini skirt or shorts. As my mother always told me, it is not the teeth that smile but the heart.

Keeping the True Me Alive

By Julia Musiime*

When I discovered my sexual orientation, it wasn't easy to accept. I was 14, and the pawpaws on my chest still didn't show through the t-shirts that I always wore with my favorite shorts during holidays. I preferred t-shirts and shorts to skirts and blouses, which made me feel I was in a wrong body – one that didn't match the inner me.

I had just moved to a new school where there were many clubs for boys and girls. Every new student longed to join the Drama Club because it had all the beautiful girls and handsome boys. It also had as its patron a young teacher nicknamed Kaboy, or "little young man," who was full of life. I attended all of the club's shows, which were spectacular, but I never joined. I opted for the girls' football club instead. I had always loved playing football. And now, with the chemistry in my body seemingly busy making and unmaking me, I found another reason to enjoy the game: I was starting to feel an attraction to the other girl players. I found myself looking at them and wondering about the shape or feel of their breasts. I started looking forward to the time we changed into our uniforms for practice or games. I would take time and allow my eyes to savor their bodies. I was always the last to finish dressing.

---

* Not the author's real name

This new attraction made me uncomfortable. I was born to a Christian mother who worked in church as a warden for as long as I can remember. My father also loved church while he lived. I prayed hard never to be discovered eyeing my female teammates because I knew the school would expel me without warning. I had heard people condemn okusiiyana, which, loosely translated, means homosexuality. The mysterious death of a human rights activist who was rumored to be promoting homosexuality evoked comments that such behavior had no place in Uganda, that it was "imported" from Europe and was very un-African.

Although I was African both in color and blood, and I had taken no flights to import the feelings welling up inside me, I felt afraid. I did not know what to do. I tried to tell my mind to stop, but it rebelled. In spite of my fear, I kept running to the bathroom after games and practices, waiting for the rest of the girls to come in and start bathing, my eyes feasting but my heart at war with itself.

I did not tell anyone about how I felt because I did not know what to say. I did not understand myself well enough. At school, many students – including most of the drama club members – were forming couples even though the school frowned on coupling. But I never felt attracted to any boy, even the many who would write me love letters on beautiful writing pads. We would play together during breaks, and generally talk as friends. And back home, I would roll down hills with boys in the grass that scratched and made my skin itch as we grazed our fathers' cows. But I never felt for them the way some of the older girls did, and I eventually lost interest in the hide-and-seek games I played with boys while grazing the cows. From now on, it would just be girls and girls and girls for me.

With this new interest, my mind took me on a journey – a journey to my future. I started picturing my life as an adult. It was bleak. It was a life without a marriage and children, a life at home with my mother and father all gray and aged. My sisters would be happily married with children. I loved children, and wanted to have my own. I felt sad and lost. My head began to bulge. I wanted to tell my friend Alexandra, but I feared she would laugh, so I decided to hold my sorrows in. Often, I would pick up my art book, sit on my bed and start doing my homework to extricate my mind from the tangle.

One day, while coming from a sports gala in town, I walked with one of my male admirers, a boy named Ronald. He proposed a short date that same evening. He said he had been eyeing me, and had a lot he wanted to share with me. For the first time in my life, I agreed to have a male-female talk. I hoped it would change the weird feelings I was having and thus save me from my distress.

We walked together. Once we reached school, we stood behind his classroom and he started telling me that he loved me. He said the boys in my class kept talking about how I played hard-to-get, but he said he knew I simply had not met someone to whom my heart belonged. The statement created a haze of confusion in my mind. I did not say a word. I did not know what to say. I just listened. When the bell for supper rang, he stopped talking and waited in silence for a minute. But instead of answering, I excused myself and headed for my hostel. When I saw him in class the following day, I knew he was upset. After that, I didn't say "yes" to a "hetero" date for some time.

Many boys in my class kept writing me letters, but I rejected them all. They could never understand the fire building inside my body. I did not blame them. Even my sisters would never understand, given our upbringing. This was a unique fire. It seemed to have come to stay, and I did not know how to handle it.

I continued to watch myself, checking to be sure I used the "right" words, associated with the "right" people, and didn't do anything "wrong." I tried to avoid being in the company of girls so as to resist the temptation of telling them how I felt. I knew my feelings were unacceptable. But my body resisted all the controlling mechanisms. I finally told Linnet, an older schoolmate, that I had feelings for her. She had a special liking for me. She slept in a different room from mine, but she spent most of her hostel time in my room with me. We talked and laughed and told stories before she went to sleep. One night, she asked whether we could share my bed for a night. I had never shared a bed at school, but I knew it was all right to share it with Linnet because we liked each other.

She came in a nightgown that was as sleek as her body, which I had been watching every day. She entered the bed, and I quickly finished what I was doing so I could join her. I rolled close to her and felt her warm, soft body on mine. I cuddled close to her. She let me. For a long time I held my breath, wondering what would happen next. I decided to move my hand like someone in sleep, and when I did, it went right to her boobs. She moved to create more space for me. But in the end, the night turned out as ordinary as any night I had spent alone. Linnet said she wasn't like me. Her closeness to me had been innocent. She was just a friend. I was disappointed. Soon, Linnet did her final exams, and I did not see her again.

As I grew older, the word homosexuality increasingly inflamed people. I heard more and more stories about overt homophobia. More stories of human rights activists dying mysteriously and of young women being gang-raped, which I knew men sometimes did to punish or "cure" lesbianism. Stories of hate filled the air. Echoing in the background were statements like, "They recruit our children into homosexuality. They deserve it." I began to hate myself. I felt that I not only lived in a frustrating body, but in a frustrating nation too. The death of one activist, David Kato, made me feel like a body living without lips; a person cannot speak of her pain or tell her story without lips. David, the lips I had hoped would free me, had been silenced.

I did not try again to be with a woman until a year after I had joined university. The atmosphere in the country kept getting worse, and I did not want to be caught in the fray. A friend of mine was raped. A man had proposed to her, and when she told him she did not have any interest in getting married soon, he attacked her one night as she returned from her campus. There were parliamentary debates on an anti-homosexuality bill.

Eventually, some calm came after the storm. The anti-homosexuality bill was set aside. People became occupied with new political issues. I was able to live my life again. During my second year at university, I met a charming woman, Bonita, with a syrupy voice and a warm, friendly manner. The first time we met, we chatted about different things – school, relationships, work and the secrets of our sexual orientation, a topic that I had long kept folded under my tongue.

But before I could fully give myself to this new-found love, I met a young man who pushed his way into my life like a heavy airplane cutting its way through the air. Bernard and I came from the same village. He was in his last year at the university, and when he came to my hostel one evening, he gave me no time to think. He said he wanted to marry me – and soon. We knew each other well, but I wondered why he wanted to move so fast. It wasn't an idea I wanted to ponder, especially so shortly after meeting Bonita.

But events were spinning out of my control. The following day, my elder sister telephoned to say she was sending me someone who needed to talk to me. "Try to be nice to him," she said at the end of the call. "I know you." She is my big sister, so I said I would be nice, even though I did not know what this man wanted from me. Later when he showed up in a white double-cabin pick-up, I discovered that my sister had sent me another potential husband. I was only 23, but my family had never seen me with boyfriends. I started wondering, "Was I too old? Was I already beginning to worry my family about when I would get married?"

Bernard kept coming to check on me. With him on one side and my sister on the other, I felt like a fish caught in a net. I did not have a way out. I had to marry. It was either Bernard or my sister's friend for a husband. Bonita was not anywhere in the picture, even though she was the person I loved. I felt suffocated. I decided to marry Bernard quickly to suppress what I felt for her. So I married him. It was just a month after I had graduated from university.

Bernard did not bring me ecstasy. During the two and a half years we were together, I lived a life that wasn't mine. I desperately wanted out. I wanted my happiness back. But our marriage had been traditional, so it would be hard to escape; if I left Bernard, my family would have to return the bride wealth his family had given us in return for me. Fortunately, by this time, I had started working, so I could pay Bernard's family back. My father had passed away a few months earlier, so I had no explanations to make to him. My mother would understand me. Still, it is not easy to end a marriage in Uganda. So I lied about Bernard, saying he had behaviours that I could not tolerate. Somehow, I managed to get away with it.

My life after marriage wasn't easy either, though. It seems I got out of one closet only to live in another. When I left the marriage, I was ready for all the disparaging things people – including my own family members – would say. But I was not ready to share my reality with them. Even though I was out of my marriage, many people still viewed being lesbian as sinful or western, so I never mentioned it to anyone.

Living in Kampala, a city many kilometers away from my home village, made it easier for me to live my life. I discovered that there were clubs and other places where I could meet with my own kind of people. Being with them gave me a sense of belonging. I started to feel appreciated for what I am. So my life became easier and a bit more meaningful, even though I remained in my second closet.

Since then, I have managed to live my life as a butch lesbian. I enjoy it when I overhear people asking each other whether I am a woman or a man; it makes me feel that I have managed to accept and live my identity. I have kept the true me alive. I don't have to be what everybody else thinks I should be. I still can exercise my humanity even if I don't foresee anyone legislating in my favor any time soon in my country.

I look forward to a time when I will be able to get out of my second closet, to live openly as the person I am. Someday, I may be confronted by a homophobic lot. I like to think the conversation may go like this:

Them (with their guns pointed at me): "Are you gay or not?"

Me (With my eyes closed): "Lord, I know some of these people may be heartless enough to send me to my rest. So I pray that you help rest my soul in eternal peace if they do. Amen!"

Them: "What? Is that the answer to the question?"

Me (Looking straight in their eyes): "Yes. I am gay."

School of Fear

By Laura Walusimbi

It was one of the darkest days of my childhood. I was in primary school, a shy, eleven-year-old eager to do well and avoid trouble. But trouble arrived anyway when my science teacher stormed into class with the results of a test the class had taken the day before. His squinty eyes were now twice their normal size. I had never seen him so upset. Obviously, we had done very poorly. He handed us our papers, and when I saw mine, my heart sank. There were so many crosses on it. I looked around the class, and could tell by the downcast faces that many students had flunked.

Then the teacher made a shocking announcement. In order to deter such poor performance on future tests, he had decided to cane each of us once for every question we got wrong. Normally, whipping was reserved for those who flunked, and even then, the shamed students would get a fixed number of strokes. This time, there would be retribution for every single error. I was horrified. My paper had numerous red crosses on every page.

Corporal punishment was common in schools in the 1970s, 1980s and 1990s. Teachers caned children who had poor grades, came late to class, talked or fidgeted in class or misbehaved. But I studied hard, and generally did well. I was never late because my family lived very near the school, and when the first bell signaled the beginning of the school day, I could tear out of the house and arrive in time to start class. As for talking in class, I was very timid, and hated to draw attention to myself, so I only spoke if the teacher addressed me directly. In short, I was the kind of student teachers usually prized. I had never been caned.

But that changed on the day of the dismal test results. When the teacher read out the first question and answer, I barely heard what he said because my heart was pounding so loudly in my ears. I watched wide-eyed as he took up his cane, and told all who had gotten the answer wrong to go to the front of the class. A bunch of students grimly shuffled forward. Some lay down on the floor, while others leaned against the blackboard with their backs to the class. Then the teacher raised the long, thin stick we all dreaded, and in one fluid movement brought it down with a loud thwack! Each student received the same stinging treatment.

When my turn came I dragged my feet as slowly as I could, all the while praying that I would miraculously disappear before I reached the front or that the teacher would somehow be spirited away. Even though I expected to be hurt, I was not prepared for the pain that coursed through my tense body when the cane fell on me. It felt like the stick split the skin on my backside. I thought I was actually bleeding. Tears welled up in my eyes as I hurried back to my desk. Another look at my answer sheet brought extra tears as I calculated how much more pain I had in store. But after the fifth or so round of beatings, I found I could dodge the teacher's repeated summonses. I figured he could not possibly know all the questions I had failed, and I was not going to help him remember.

After the teacher was finished, my backside burned hot and raw. The psychic pain was at least as bad. I was humiliated and angry -- humiliated because the teacher made me feel daft when I knew I was not and because my shame had been laid bare before all my classmates, and angry because the teacher had overreacted and chosen a brutal form of punishment. That was the first time I had failed his subject. Besides, almost half the class had failed the test, which should have told him something about the test itself – or about his own failings as a teacher. He should have dug deeper to understand why we failed instead of resorting to this beastly punishment. Did he really think we deliberately failed the test? Did getting the wrong answers reflect a moral failing on our part?

There seemed to be no answer to my bewildered questions. Yet even now, more than three decades later, I vividly recall that incident and resent the pain and helplessness I felt the day when a person who was older and stronger wounded my body and shattered my dignity. It seemed so senseless.

In my day, school was synonymous with fear. The focus was on passing exams, and terror was the tool teachers used to make sure we never lost sight of that goal. Sometimes, as many as six teachers lined up to give two strokes of the cane to each pupil who failed an exam. Some students were caned so frequently that they routinely lined their underwear with cotton, extra underwear and other padding to reduce the pain. While caning was supposed to be a corrective measure, some teachers went overboard, appearing to relish it. You could tell how vindictive they were by how they hit; some whipped us in a controlled manner, while others thrashed wildly all over our bodies, including our heads.

People who were caned rarely improved in either their schoolwork or their behavior. Most seemed resigned to their fate. It's little wonder. Parents accepted the notion that caning was the best way to get children to excel in their studies. They often quoted the Biblical verse, "Spare the rod and spoil the child." After all, they had been brought up the same way. In my father's first year in primary school, a teacher once caned him with a huge stick until it broke. His crime? He got to school late that morning. When he became a parent, my father only spanked us once (and when he explained the reasons, we agreed that we deserved it).

But parents like my father were rare. I had many aunts and uncles who believed that the rod worked wonders in instilling discipline in children. And several of my peers, especially the ones who went to primary boarding schools, recall their time at school with anything but fondness. One of my cousins once ended up with three blood clots in her fingers after a teacher caned her. When the teacher was whipping her, she had instinctively tried to protect herself with her hands.

By the time I reached adulthood, corporal punishment was out of control. One national paper wrote that the practice had degenerated into "random and irresponsible beating of students by the teachers and fellow students." In August 2006, the same paper carried a story about five students in a secondary school who had been hospitalized after they were severely beaten by a group of teachers. The disciplining had turned into a torture session. Had the teachers taken the biblical verse and corporal punishment to an unjustified extreme? Or was the problem that our school system was sending undertrained and underpaid teachers into overcrowded classrooms, and then putting so much pressure on them to produce students who scored well on national tests that their frustration grew to destructive levels? Or was it simply that in many schools there were few, if any, controls to monitor teachers' behavior?

I don't know the answer. But I do know this: Often when a teacher caned a child to instill discipline, the punishment was not so much about discipline as power – a desire to show the child who was in control.

I often wonder what long-term effects such abuse has on children as they grow to adulthood. Surely, children who were physically abused must grow up lacking self-esteem and viewing people in authority with a mix of fear and resentment. What is even more worrisome is that many such children end up as teachers. What are the chances that they will repeat the cycle? How much of today's violence was actually learned in school?

The situation eventually took a turn for the better – at least somewhat. In 2006, the Ministry of Education banned corporal punishment in all schools, from nursery school to college. Perhaps we had reached a turning point.

Unfortunately, the government didn't vigorously enforce the ban, so caning continues in many schools. In 2011, an advocacy group reported that 81% of pupils in central and northern Uganda were still being beaten at school. The same year, I witnessed a teacher beat a child. When I asked why she did it, the teacher said, without batting an eyelid, that the child was stupid and deserved it. Besides, she argued, if she did not beat students, they would remain "stubborn."

At the same time, a more sinister form of punishment has cropped up – verbal and psychological lashing. Often when I pass by schools – nursery, primary, or secondary – I overhear teachers hurling abuse at children. Students imitate their teachers, and mete out similar abuse, spewing comments like "You're stupid," "You won't amount to anything," and "You fool" at each other. Also, many adults have an ugly habit of pushing children's heads at the temple – an act that is degrading, can be painful and, I suspect, leaves the same residue of self-doubt and resentment that follows physical abuse.

Change comes slowly. For years, I, like most parents, thought it was normal to cane since that is the way I was brought up. But my outlook changed once I started a family. My first child was a hyper toddler who loved to run around and play with anything he got his hands on. Well-meaning relatives advised that if I did not cane him, he would become unmanageable. So I tried spanking him, but the more I hit him, the more defiant he became. I soon realized that caning did not achieve sustainable results, and I understood how it can get out of hand. Indeed, I was wracked with guilt each time I physically punished one of my children. Beating hurts not only the children but also the beater. So I stopped. I now prefer to use other methods of instilling discipline in my children. When they were younger I used timeouts, a "naughty corner" and other less violent methods. I now talk to them more and explain that there are consequences when they misbehave. If they act up, they know there will be punishment like being grounded or having a favorite toy or gadget confiscated for a period of time.

Today, more and more schools are enforcing the caning ban. Perhaps it has something to do with the mushrooming number of schools. Parents have more choices about where to send their children. We still have the traditional schools, both privately owned and government-run, that follow the national curriculum and focus on academic performance and strict discipline, sometimes including clandestine caning. But international schools, which generally are more interested in a holistic education for the pupils, are growing steadily in number. And there also are private schools that try to incorporate the best of both the national and international schools.

My sons' first primary school officially frowned on caning, and relied instead on less harsh forms of punishment. Talkative or hyperactive students were sent to stand in different classes for a specified amount of time. The embarrassment and trouble of having to catch up with class work afterwards were enough to discourage disobedience. More importantly, teachers encouraged children to understand what they were learning instead of just memorizing it. The school encourages physical, spiritual and mental development as well as academic studies. And rather than beating children for bad behavior or poor performance, it holds an annual ceremony to reward children who have excelled in different disciplines – academics, music, sports and general behavior. All the children yearn to be on the list. That alone motivates many to do better.

Perhaps teachers also need the incentive of annual award ceremonies to treat their students sensitively.

While some teachers are genuinely interested in guiding pupils to become better people, they are the minority. Many teachers still shout at their students to get them to do their bidding. How long before that ceases to have an impact and the teacher who uses that method resorts to other ways of "disciplining"? To make matters worse, many teachers today carry grudges against their schools' management or the government – anger they often take out on children. Sometimes the anger is about the low pay they get. Sometimes it may result from frustrations borne out of the lack of proper training. And sometimes teachers succumb to the notion that school is all about grades – a one-dimensional, dehumanizing view that can set the stage for physical abuse.

It begins with pumping students with tons of homework throughout the week, on every weekend and even during holidays.

Forget critical thinking; the children do the same thing over and over again. Is it any surprise that teachers with so little imagination and such a dim view of students can think of nothing better than caning when all the homework fails to produce the test results they seek?

A more compassionate – and effective – approach should begin with the recognition that school is not all about the grades. Teachers should not just help children improve academically but should help them become well-rounded people. Such an approach can improve many aspects of student performance – even grades. Once, my son enrolled in an after-school football club at his school. He loves football with a passion (what boy doesn't?). Unfortunately, his grades slipped. His teacher immediately blamed football, and urged my husband and me to take him out of the program. We did, but his grades slipped further because he was miserable. We later learned that football wasn't the problem at all. He was having difficulties adjusting to the new class and new teacher. So we allowed him to go back to football, and since then not only have his grades improved but he is also doing very well in football.

Maybe problems like corporal punishment keep arising because we don't give teachers the help they need. I try as much as I can to attend school events – parent-teacher conferences, concerts, school assemblies (the ones parents are invited to) and sports days. I often check in with the teachers so I know how my children are doing in class. Many of the other parents do the same. We believe working hand in hand with the teachers and school management will go a long way toward getting the children better treatment and a decent education.

But it's a struggle. Many teachers are defensive, and see parental involvement as a threat. Two years ago, my son came home and told me the teacher had announced that they were having a school assembly and all the sports students were going to be awarded. She then singled him and a couple other pupils out and told them not to tell their parents about it, presumably because she didn't want us to attend the assembly. I was stunned.

Incompetent teachers blame anyone but themselves for their failure. One teacher in my sons' school thought that all the boys in her class were unmanageable. Everything that went wrong – poor performance of the whole class, noise in class or whatever – was because of the boys. To me that was a clear admission of failure.

We finally pulled our children out of that school. I had had enough – of the poor teaching methods, the double standards, the lack of follow up and the steady migration of good teachers to other schools. The final straw was when a group of good teachers left en masse to join an international school. It happens in other schools too. I never understood why some parents in my generation move their children from one school to another. Now, I know. They want the best opportunity for their children. So do I.

But good schools are hard to find. If they are not expensive then they compromise on too many things. For a while, I considered home schooling. But there was one sticking point: how would I ensure that my boys did not end up in a social no man's land, unable to interact effectively with people of different ages and backgrounds?

We finally found a better school. It is smaller, with a more favorable pupil-to-teacher ratio. Its teachers are well trained and more motivated to teach. The children respond in kind by working hard and being committed to the school. Although the teachers are strict, they also are friendly. The relationship between the teacher and the pupil (and by extension, the parents) is cordial. It no longer feels as though the teachers are against us.

I worry a lot less. The threat of corporal punishment may be receding. But there are so many new challenges and no easy answers.

The Authors

Harriet Anena is a poet and writer from Gulu, Uganda. The author of "A Nation in Labour," a poetry collection, her poems and short stories have been widely published. In 2013, she was shortlisted for the Ghana Poetry Prize. She finds great pleasure in bullying words for poetic pleasure.

Caroline Ariba is a features writer with The New Vision, a newspaper based in Kampala, Uganda. Hailing all the way from the eastern district of Kumi in Uganda's Teso region, she dreams of a career in travel where from she can experience and write about different cultures.

Sophie Nuwagira Bamwoyeraki was born in south-western Uganda, but now lives in Kampala, where she works as a teacher of English and literature in an international school. She is a member of Uganda Women Writers' Association FEMRITE. She writes short stories and poetry.

Elvania M. Bazaala is a freelance architect born and raised in the suburbs of Kampala. Her greatest weaknesses are sports and chocolate. She believes that the happenstances of life are the reason this world is colorful.

Shifa Mwesigye is a journalist, science writer and blogger. She has won a number of awards, including recognition from the CNN Multichoice African Journalism Awards. She is a mother of wonderful twins and spends her spare time trying to award equal attention to them as they vie for her undivided attention.

Lydia Namubiru is a journalist based in Kampala, Uganda, and mother of a brilliant daughter, Hailey. A graduate of Makerere University, she is a program associate for the African Center for Media Excellence. She has worked as a newspaper reporter and program analyst for international nongovernment organizations.

Nakisanze Segawa is a performance poet working in Luganda, her native language. She has published poems and short stories in English and Luganda, and recently completed her first novel. Spiritually, she has gone back to her roots, and is a fully converted adherent to African traditional religion.

Rosey Sembatya loves words and dogs. She has a short story, "Nine Lives," to her name, published in a collection entitled "Summoning the Rains" (2012). Rosey manages an education consultancy that compiles interactive learning texts for students.

 *Peace Twine holds a Master of Arts degree with post-graduate training in gender, human/women's rights. A teacher by profession, she worked with civil society, is a director of a secondary school and a member of a number of organizations at national and regional levels. She is a grandmother.*

Hilda Twongyeirwe is a founding member of Femrite, the Uganda Women Writers Association. She is also a member of other art and cultural initiatives. She is a published writer of short stories and children's books. She is passionate about women and children's issues. Hilda is mother of one daughter and two sons.

 *Laura M. Walusimbi lives in Kampala, Uganda. She is married and has been blessed with two precious boys. She now works as a freelance journalist and consulting editor. Her greatest desire is to see that her children enjoy their school years.*

Ronnie Ogwang is a professional visual artist with a Bachelor of Arts in Industrial Fine Arts and design from Makerere University. He has had exhibitions in Uganda, Kenya, Australia and Germany, and has worked for the US National Library of Medicine and the Central Bank of Uganda. He loves to paint the female figure, and believes that women are the most important part of society.

Christopher Conte is a writer, editor and journalism teacher based in Washington, DC. A former reporter and editor for the Wall Street Journal, he has reported and trained journalists on health, economic, social issues and writing. He lived in Uganda from 2008 through 2010, and considers the country his second home.